BACKROADS *of*
*S*OUTHERN *C*ALIFORNIA

Bob Howells

Gulf Publishing Company

To Michael,
to my fellow pilgrims,
and to Katherine, my love.

Gulf Publishing Company
Book Division
P. O. Box 2608 □ Houston, Texas 77252-2608

10 9 8 7 6 5 4 3 2 1

Library of Congress Cataloging-in-Publication Data
Howells, Bob
  Backroads of Southern California / Bob Howells.
      p. cm.
  Includes index.
  ISBN 0-88415-146-8
  1. California, Southern—Guidebooks. 2. Automobile
travel—California, Southern—Guidebooks. I. Title.
F867.H78 1995
917.94′90453—dc20   94-46116
                                                 CIP

Printed in the United States of America.

Contents

v

Introduction

Southern California often takes a bashing from cultural and geographical snobs who damn the entire region for consorting with metropolitan Los Angeles. They assume it's one giant urban wasteland cloaked in smog, born yesterday with no link to the past, and lulled senseless by perennially perfect weather.

In the course of many years of traveling and travel writing, I've been a quiet defender of my homeland, staunchly muttering such halfhearted proclamations as, "Hey, it's not such a bad place," while I've spent much of my time traveling away from it and writing about any place but the one I call home.

It's time to stop muttering. Southern California is blessed by nature and even by mankind. The profound geographical lures that have brought so many to this region are still intact, frequently untrammeled, and surprisingly accessible. Even a brief exploration of Southern California's backroads reveals dimensions hidden from casual observers. Deeper exploration—that is, a lot of backroads rambling—brings even greater rewards. The process of researching this book, exploring my native terrain, and making countless discoveries and rediscoveries has been a great pleasure, and an even greater pleasure to share.

Anyone who follows a chapter of this book will know immediately that Southern California is not Los Angeles. "An island on the land," Helen Hunt Jackson called it, and like any good island, Southern California is laced with an exotic landscape that kindles dreams and an energy that lures visionaries and loonies in equal measure. Many of them have ended up in Los Angeles, but as much as L.A. is bursting at its seams, the city is but a large speck on the Southern California landscape, and its freeways are but a gossamer snare. There's another life and landscape just an off-ramp away.

An hour or two away from the freeway din, I can sit in the shade of a palm oasis, dangle my toes in a pool of water, peer through the palms at the hefty shank of a snow-covered mountain, and hear nothing but the crinkly rustle of palm fronds and the twittering of invisible birds. If I'd just clunked 2,400 miles along the Butterfield Overland stage route, I'd feel pretty well rewarded for my ordeal. That such places are right outside my car door makes me feel blessed to live in Southern California in the 20th century.

Sure its history is brief, but there's plenty to stimulate nostalgic reveries along the backroads of Southern California: Small towns like Julian that serve up tasty homemade apple pie and friendly conversation, or Ballard, with its one-room schoolhouse surrounded by horse farms. When I step out of my car into such places, I feel that I've stepped out of the 1990s and into 1910. And if I find myself longing for days when not everything was prefabbed, cookie-cuttered, and focused-grouped into dulling sameness of taste and appearance, I can find plenty of vestiges of individuality, quirkiness, and downright oddness along the backroads. I can roll in to the Grubstake Inn in Landers for a tasty hunk of meat loaf and visit the nearby Integratron, a whitewashed wooden dome purportedly inspired by alien beings. I can visit roadside "auctions" of fascinating junk in places like Lucerne Valley, Oro Grande, and Los Alamos. I can spurn the chain motels and bed down at the four-room Hotel Nipton, where a sign in my chamber warns, "This room is equipped with Edison electric light. Do not attempt to light. Simply turn key by door." And if I'm feeling hemmed in by the city, I don't have to venture far to revel in unspoiled spaciousness. I can leave a San Diego beach, and in an hour I'm driving the spine of the Laguna Mountains, sussing out viewpoints of the Anza-Borrego Desert far below. Twenty minutes from downtown Los Angeles I can wind my way into the San Gabriel Mountains along the Angeles Crest Highway. I can day-trip up to Santa Barbara County and find poppy-lined roads winding through a timeless landscape of California oaks and tall grasses.

There's a place in the Providence Mountains of the East Mojave Desert where I can drive to a viewpoint, look down upon hundreds of square miles of open space, and see virtually nothing man-made. It just happens that the view takes in an area about the same size as the entire Los Angeles basin. If I linger there till dusk, I can watch the stars reclaim the sky and the Milky Way emerge as it does in astronomical photos. Below, in the L.A.-sized basin, I do see one, maybe two, lights come on in the distance. I know I'm not alone, because what has lured me here has also brought others. That has always been the way in Southern California.

Nor am I alone in chronicling the backroads of Southern California. I hold in esteem at least two who preceded me: Joseph Smeaton Chase, the intrepid Englishman who scoured California's desert and coast by horseback in the second decade of the century, and Russ Leadabrand, whose 1960s books and articles in *Westways* magazine helped guide and inspire me.

One of the pleasures of driving the backroads of Southern California is dallying with the ghosts of those who have come before—at places like the Vallecito Stage Station in Anza-Borrego, the long-abandoned gas stations and motels of old Route 66, and the forlorn towns that fringe the Salton Sea. You'll find many such ghosts in these pages, but the book is not really about what has gone away. It's about what is still here. Researching it and writing it felt like a celebration of great beauty, history, life, and spaciousness in a place presumed by the snobs to have none of these. If you run into ghosts along your backroads travels, thank them for paving the way and leaving us with so much to explore.

ABOUT THE TOURS

Each chapter of *Backroads of Southern California* is designed as a driving tour along routes easily traveled by any average sedan. If time is short, any one tour can be driven in a day. A weekend is better, and two or three days will really get you into the spirit of backroads exploration. Some tours are loops. Others don't quite close the loop, but leave you poised to either head off on another tour or return to your starting point.

Southern California has no official boundaries, but one thing is for certain: You don't fold a California map in half and call the bottom part Southern California. The state is just too vertical to impose such an arbitrary boundary. The limits of Southern California are more dictated by tradition, a sense that has been passed down like folklore. "My" Southern California lies below the county lines of San Luis Obispo and Kern, and south of Death Valley to the Mexican border. Hence the book comprises eight counties: San Diego, Imperial, San Bernardino, Riverside, Orange, Los Angeles, Ventura, and Santa Barbara.

With apologies to non-Angelenos, directions to these driving tours presume Los Angeles as a starting place. I needed a reference point, and Los Angeles seemed to be a logical one. With decent maps, it should be easy to adjust the directions to suit your point of origin. Speaking of maps, those included with each chapter are useful for reference, but I urge you to pick up more detailed maps for your explorations. For my travels, I used the county maps published by the Automobile Club of Southern California, which are available free to members of the American Automobile Association (AAA). These contain just the right amount of detail for these tours—virtually every road I've described is shown on the Auto Club's county maps.

With few exceptions, I've stayed to paved roads. Four-wheel drive is not necessary for any of these tours. Even RVs should be able to negotiate these backroads routes easily. The going can be slow in the East Mojave, but even the dirt roads I've suggested there are traversable by two-wheel drive and RVs.

There's certainly nothing official or sacrosanct about the routes I've described here. Travel them as I have, and you'll enjoy great drives, scenic vistas, and small, friendly towns. You'll encounter historical sites and, if my affinity for quirky places appeals to you, you'll find lots of fodder for wonderment and chuckles. If you use the tours as touchstones to lead you into an area from which you follow your own whims and intuition, then you're really into the spirit of backroads driving, and I'd love to hear about your discoveries.

I don't intend this book to be a dining or lodging guide, although I've described some places of exceptional character along the way. I do tell you the best place to get an ostrich burger and where you can sleep in a Cadillac and watch "drive-in" movies. But again, your own discoveries may well be your most treasured memories as you explore the backroads of Southern California.

TOUR 1

Santa Barbara Backroads

110 Miles
*Lake Casitas • Casitas Pass • Carpinteria • Montecito •
Mountain Drive • Santa Barbara • San Marcos Pass •
Camino Cielo • Cold Spring Canyon • Paradise*

"America's Riviera," some call it, but Santa Barbara
doesn't need the European analogy. Quite on its own, it is
one of the loveliest cities in America. It spreads out over a
narrow plain that slopes from the base of the Santa Ynez
Mountains to the placid waters of the Santa Barbara
Channel—a confetti of whitewashed stucco and red tile,
palm trees, avocados, and coast live oak. The city has long
been a favored weekend escape for Angelenos seeking to
clear their lungs and find a good meal or to prowl the city's
paseos, parks, bookstores, and beaches. However, my
intent is not to offer a sightseeing guide to Santa Barbara,
but to suggest an alternative way to get there and some
backroads to explore that originate in Santa Barbara and
radiate into the mountains that form its backdrop. These
should offer a new perspective for anyone fond of Santa
Barbara—and who isn't?

To begin the tour: Take Highway 101 west to Ventura and go north on State Highway 33 toward Ojai. Instead of continuing into Ojai, turn left on Santa Ana Boulevard (stoplight) in the unincorporated hamlet of Oak View.

You're immediately in a rural setting of horse farms, ramshackle old barns, and a crossroads country store—you know, the kind that sells Spam and earthworms. Turn right at the country store intersection on Santa Ana Road, follow it up a rise (which offers a good view of the Ojai Valley), and you come upon the northeastern corner of Lake Casitas.

LAKE CASITAS

Drought is a way of life in this part of Southern California, which does not draw on the State Water Project flow from the north nor the Colorado River from the east. When Casitas Dam was completed in 1959, it was thought to be a hedge against drought for local residents and citrus farmers. The lake draws from a watershed of 105 square miles, but even so, its level drops greatly during years of prolonged drought. Summers are always hot and dry here, but during a drought year, the desiccated shoreline makes the whole place look pretty haggard. In wetter years it's a wonderful spot to picnic, camp, or fish. (Because the lake is a domestic water supply, swimming and waterskiing are not allowed.) It just may have the best fishing in Southern California, with such prodigious records as a 21-pound bass, 42-pound catfish, 3.6-pound crappie, and 9.25-pound trout. The county park that surrounds it has all the usual amenities such as boat rentals, snack bar, and camp store.

Santa Ana Road skirts the lake and leads to the main entrance, where you'll need to pay a day-use fee to enter. If you go into the park and bear left, you'll come to the site of the rowing events for the 1984 Olympic Games. Just beyond the park entrance is the junction of State Highway 150. Turn left here, and you'll climb above the lake's northern shoreline and get a good view of the island in its center. After a semiloop around the west side, Highway 150 leaves the lake and takes off up Casitas Pass, then snakes down steeply into a region of backwoods avocado farms.

CARPINTERIA

Where Highway 150 meets State Highway 192, take the right fork on Highway 192 which leads into the inland side of the pleasant beach town of Carpinteria. The commercial center and beach ("the world's safest," the town claims) are

Lake Casitas and rugged, chaparral-covered mountains are among the scenic highlights along Highway 150, the backroad from Ojai to Carpinteria.

a little bit to the south. This side of Carpinteria is completely given over to horticulture—huge greenhouses of orchids and roses, groves of lemons and avocados, fields of statice and baby's breath, and ornamental eucalyptus. Most of the operations sell only to wholesalers, but a few welcome the public on certain days of the week. One, Stewart Orchids, welcomes visitors every day.

Carpinteria is a Spanish word meaning carpenter's shop. The Chumash Indians who lived on this plain were expert canoe builders, and they utilized natural tar deposits in the area to seal the canoes. Spanish soldiers in Gaspar de Portola's 1769 expedition supposedly saw the Indians' canoe workshop and gave the place its name.

Highway 192, now appropriately called Foothill Road, cuts through the commercial nurseries, then makes a jog to the right at the edge of the Santa Barbara Polo and Racquet Club. You can't see inside to the polo field—it's hidden by a tall hedge—but visitors are welcome to watch the Sunday afternoon matches from April through October.

MONTECITO

The highway undergoes a series of name changes as it climbs up Toro Canyon, then resumes its western course as East Valley Road through opulent Montecito. You needn't feel like a voyeur as you pass through this haven for the extremely wealthy because most of the estates are gated, hedged, and walled. Gawk all you want—you can't see much. But you get the idea—gentry horse farms, mansions, tennis courts, and money. A lot of money.

Montecito began as a resort for the wealthy, who were attracted to its weather and hot springs. Scions such as Armstrong, Du Pont, Fleischman, Pillsbury, and Stetson built Montecito mansions early in the century. These days,

Highway 192 passes through the oaks and opulence of Montecito, where horse farms and grand estates lurk behind split-rail fences and tall walls.

the denizens are more likely to be entertainment industry stars and moguls, but discretion prevails—don't expect to see kids selling maps to the stars' homes.

East Valley Road continues through the heart of Montecito and changes its name a few more times on the way to Santa Barbara. But I suggest an alternative route that follows a higher contour along the base of the Santa Ynez Mountains, a way that offers some stunning views of homes, canyons, and the ocean.

Turn right in Montecito on San Ysidro Road (stoplight) and bear right on San Ysidro Lane, which leads into San Ysidro Ranch, the Santa Barbara area's most romantic hideaway hotel. That John and Jackie Kennedy chose to honeymoon here should tell you something. Guests stay in white cottages surrounded by lawns and gardens and dine in Stonehouse Restaurant, which is also open to nonguests. The 525-acre ranch backs onto national forest land, so it's utterly private and quiet. Even if you don't intend to stay, it's worth making the quick loop in and out of San Ysidro Ranch, which will deposit you heading west on Mountain Drive.

Mountain Drive

Mountain Drive, a wonderful road full of potholes and devoid of lane markers, twists tortuously along the Santa Ynez foothills. A number of S-bends jut out over south-facing slopes, affording views across ranches, canyons, and ever more opulent neighborhoods toward Santa Barbara Harbor. Be alert as you drive for a couple of stone-arch bridges—Troll Bridge and Coyote Bridge—both built with beautiful stone craftsmanship circa 1880.

Finally, after dozens of tight zigzags, Mountain Drive drops down to rejoin Highway 192, which has now reacquired the name Foothill Road. Turn right on Foothill Road. You'll soon come to Mission Canyon Road, where you can turn right to visit the Santa Barbara Botanic Garden—a

Santa Barbara Mission is the city's landmark building. The mission was completed in 1820 and rebuilt after a 1925 earthquake.

delightful showcase for California native plants and a great spot for an easy hike. Or turn left on Mission Canyon to visit the famous Santa Barbara Mission. The 1820 building is, I think, the most lovely of California missions—a striking structure surrounded by lawns and a rose garden.

But I wasn't going to be your guide to Santa Barbara. So once you've visited the mission and the city, return up Mission Canyon Road to Foothill Road and continue west (left) to the junction of State Highway 154.

SAN MARCOS PASS

As you proceed north on State Highway 154, an officially designated state scenic highway, you climb from near sea level to 2,224 feet. The rugged hills are coated in thick chaparral—mottled much of the year with brilliant wildflowers, particularly the abundant bush sunflower. This, the San

Marcos Pass through the Santa Ynez Mountains, is a route that carried many a stagecoach traveler and, earlier, Colonel John C. Frémont's California battalion en route to destiny in Santa Barbara. Frémont descended the semi-secret pass on Christmas Day in 1846 during the American conquest of California, surprising a band of Mexicans who had earlier overrun a small American garrison.

Of course, the pass and these mountains had long been known to the native Chumash Indians. One of the best-preserved examples of Chumash cave art is located up a steep, narrow side road worth a brief detour. Turn right on Painted Cave Road and follow it to Chumash Painted Cave State Historic Park. Watch carefully—one small sign and a couple of turnouts on this very narrow road are your only clues to the presence of the cave. The cave is just a few yards up a rocky trail from the road. Although it's dark in the grotto and bars have been placed to protect it from vandals, the paintings are vivid—swirls, geometrics, horned animals, and humans. They were probably made over the course of many years by Chumash shamans, whom the Indians believed could communicate with supernatural forces. They painted symbols to influence the supernatural and, possibly, also to record important events. Some experts believe that a sun painting represents a seventeenth-century total eclipse of the sun.

Beyond the cave, this road continues to climb steeply through a little settlement called, naturally, Painted Cave, and finally meets East Camino Cielo— "the sky road."

THE SKY ROAD

If you turn left on East Camino Cielo, you'll soon intersect with Highway 154 and resume the ultimate course of this tour. But turn right to take one of the most spectacular roads anywhere that leads nowhere. Camino Cielo is a narrow, often steep and potholed road that follows the

View of Knapp's Castle from East Camino Cielo. George Owen Knapp's dream retreat in the Santa Ynez Mountains was destroyed by fire in 1940.

windswept, craggy crest of the front range of the Santa Ynez Mountains. It climbs and winds for 15 miles to a locked gate at Romero Saddle where you have no choice but to turn around. Stunning views continually unfold— south over Santa Barbara, Santa Barbara Channel, and the Channel Islands and north into the wild Santa Barbara backcountry, part of the wide-flung Los Padres National Forest. The road's apex is at La Cumbre Peak, 3,985 feet.

Even if you don't follow the entire Camino Cielo, I suggest a brief venture: Turn right and follow it a mile or so to a locked gate on the left. Park here to sample some of those stunning coastal views and to take a short (half-mile), fascinating hike to the ruins of a rich man's dream castle. George Owen Knapp was the former chairman of the board of Union Carbide. He built a sandstone mansion on this remote site. Although the castle burned in 1940, you can poke among the foundations, stone walls, and chimneys and muse over the magnificence of the site and what Knapp's Castle must have been like.

Return west now on East Camino Cielo. Just before you reach Highway 154 you can stop in at Cielo Store, a pleasant country market where there's likely to be an arrangement of fresh fruit on the counter next to the beef jerky and licorice twists.

COLD SPRING—TAVERN AND BRIDGE

At the junction of Highway 154, turn right. You'll quickly crest the pass, but don't be in too great a hurry. Watch for Stagecoach Road and turn left, then bear right into a lush dell that is the site of Cold Spring Tavern. Along the way, you'll get a glimpse of the Cold Spring Arch Bridge by which Highway 154 crosses Cold Spring Canyon. Its graceful structure is high (400 feet) above the canyon floor, but travelers on the highway have no sense of its swooping steel supporting arch that bridges the canyon in a single, 700-foot span.

Cold Spring Arch Bridge crosses Cold Spring Canyon in a single 700-foot span, 400 feet above the canyon floor.

Stagecoach Road follows the old stagecoach route from the Santa Ynez Valley to Santa Barbara. Six-horse coaches made this run from 1861 to 1901. Even after the end of the stagecoach era, this narrow canyon road was the way to cross Cold Spring Canyon until the bridge was completed in 1963. The first building on the site was a bunkhouse for the Chinese laborers who built the turnpike road through San Marcos Pass. The first tavern/hotel opened in 1886, and Cold Spring Tavern, in various incarnations, has served travelers on the route ever since. It obviously was a very welcome stop on the jaw-jarring, eight-hour ride between Mattei's Tavern in Los Olivos and downtown Santa Barbara. Some 52 cold artesian springs surround the tavern, so it was also the ideal place to change and water horses. Today, it's a wonderful hideaway in three parts—rustic tavern, restaurant (steaks, ribs, burgers), and gift shop ("Treasures & Trash—Open by Appointment or by Chance").

PARADISE VALLEY

From Cold Spring Tavern, continue descending the canyon on Stagecoach Road. You'll soon come to a worm's-eye view of Cold Spring Arch Bridge, looming 400 feet above. The road ultimately rejoins Highway 154. But don't pass up this chance to see Paradise—turn right on Paradise Road. This road parallels the winding Santa Ynez River for 11 miles and leads to some fine, uncrowded Los Padres National Forest campsites and picnic areas. The road fords the river several times—never a problem in summer or fall; and even in winter or spring, the water is generally just a few inches deep at these crossings. But along the way you'll find some wonderful swimming holes. The best of these is at road's end beside Live Oak picnic area. It's an old-fashioned vision of paradise—a lazy river, a cool pool, an oak-shaded valley framed by 3,000-foot peaks.

Paradise Valley of the Santa Ynez River earns its name, seen here from Highway 154 with the back ranges of the Santa Ynez Mountains forming the backdrop.

From the end of Paradise Road you have no choice but to retrace your route. You needn't turn up Stagecoach Road, though. Just beyond Paradise Store, Paradise Road intersects Highway 154. Turn right to join Tour 2 of the Santa Ynez Valley, which picks up from this spot, or left to cross Cold Spring Arch Bridge and return to Santa Barbara.

TOUR 2

Santa Ynez Valley 1: Mountains and Wineries

120 miles
San Marcos Pass • Lake Cachuma • Figueroa Mountain •
Santa Ynez • Ballard • Los Olivos • Foxen Canyon •
Zaca Lake • Sisquoc

The Santa Ynez Valley is both wild and refined at the same time. It's a place where well-heeled city slickers become country squires. They raise horses, make wine, or build indulgent retreats. But the valley is also genuine ranch country that still retains a touch of the Old West. On its north side, roads lead into the San Rafael Mountains where it's primitive and rugged but also delicate, for these slopes offer wildflower shows of dazzling beauty. Other country roads are gentler and wander through horse farms and vineyards.

The Santa Ynez Valley has so many wonderful backroads that I've divided it into two different tours. This first one takes in the wild, mountainous side and then visits wineries, staying all the while to the east of U.S. Highway 101. Tour 3 includes the tourist magnet of Solvang and wanders through the hilly country west of the freeway.

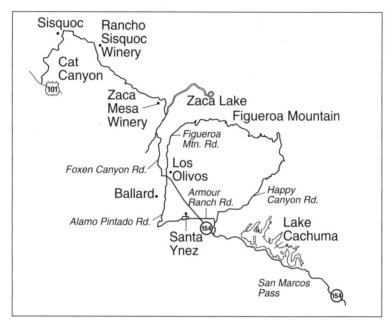

To begin the tour: Start where Tour 1 left off in the San Marcos Pass area north of Santa Barbara. Or, to begin from Los Angeles, take U.S. Highway 101 north (the predominant direction is actually west) to Santa Barbara, then State Highway 154 north through the San Marcos Pass.

State Highway 154 earns its "scenic highway" status easily and instantly, from its climb out of Santa Barbara, through the scrub oak chaparral hills, to the oak woodlands of San Marcos Pass, and down into the oak-studded meadows of the Santa Ynez Valley. Soon after cresting the pass, the roadside reveals views of two of the valley's guises amid a landscape that the Mexican ranchers called *potrero*— fields of wild oats and barley, punctuated with coast live oaks. This is virtually the trademark landscape of Southern California, and the Santa Ynez Valley has some of its most striking examples. A portion of the valley west of Paradise Road is absolutely archetypal, and, because there's a scenic overlook above it, frequently photographed. Archetypal, maybe, but the grasses we see in most of Southern California's oak woodlands are not native—they found their way here as seeds in hay bales brought by the Spanish to feed on-board livestock. Once the settlers landed, their cattle preferred to munch the native bunchgrasses. The non-native wild oats, barley, and filaree took hold and grew unchecked, and eventually overwhelmed the native grasses. The ubiquitous wild mustard flowers that splash springtime yellow all over Southern California's coastal hills are also introduced invaders.

LAKE CACHUMA

A little farther west is another guise of the Santa Ynez Valley—a watery one. Lake Cachuma is a reservoir created in 1953 when Bradbury Dam was built across the Santa Ynez River. The 3,000-acre lake is the primary water source for Santa Barbara County and the centerpiece of a 6,600-acre county park. Highway 154 skirts the lake for several miles before reaching the entrance to the park, which has excellent camping and picnicking sites, a marina, store, nature center, and excellent fishing. The lake is stocked with rainbow trout and has generous populations of bass, crappie, perch, channel catfish, and bluegill. At one time, sizable runs of spawning steelhead trout made their way up the Santa Ynez River, but human thirst and Bradbury Dam put an end to that.

Still, wildlife flourishes around Cachuma. Ranger Neil Taylor conducts excellent weekend nature cruises that are especially popular in winter, when large numbers of bald and golden eagles feed here and various ducks and wintering birds are on the water. At other times of year, you might see newborn fawns near the shore or nests of great blue herons and red-tail hawks.

If you choose not to visit the lake, you can still turn off at an observation point at the west end—the view takes in Bradbury Dam, much of the lake, and the rugged San Rafael Mountains that stand above it.

FIGUEROA MOUNTAIN

All along Highway 154, particularly the stretch west of Lake Cachuma, you can see bright golden poppies dancing in the eddies of automobile turbulence. California's state flower grows among grasses in the meadows, but particularly flourishes in the dusty road cuts along the edge of the asphalt. This is only a warm-up to the wonderful wildflower spectacle taking place on the higher ground to the north. For admission to this show, turn right on Armour Ranch Road and take the next two rights to Happy Canyon Road, a narrow ribbon of (mostly) asphalt that ascends Figueroa Mountain. In spring, you'll see huge splotches of yellow mustard in the canyons and on the slopes to the east; along the road are fields of blue lupine, poppies, and cream cups. Evidence of a fire that swept through here in 1993 will remain a long time, but where it scarred many oaks, pines, and spruce trees, it also in effect fertilized the fields—the grasses and wildflowers grow more abundantly than ever.

Figueroa Mountain has a showy variety of wildflowers anyway, as you'll discover on a hike on any of the Los Padres National Forest Trails near its summit. At the top of Happy Valley Road where it meets Figueroa Mountain Road, you can pick up a trail map at the Cachuma Saddle ranger station then proceed north on Sunset Valley Road to the Davy Brown trailhead. Or, you can turn left on Figueroa Mountain Road and pick up the same trail five miles later. It leads to a fire road that reaches Figueroa Lookout atop the peak, 4,528 feet high. Along the way, you might see johnny jump-ups, shooting stars, and Indian paintbrush. Even when the wildflowers aren't so abundant, you can walk among tall pines, firs, and riparian maple and laurel trees and enjoy panoramic views—of the Santa Ynez Valley, Cachuma, and even the Pacific.

The rugged country north and west of Figueroa Mountain is the San Rafael Wilderness Area, which became the country's first designated wilderness after Congress passed the Wilderness Act of 1964. To sample this wild backcountry, take Sunset Valley Road (at the top of Happy Canyon) to NIRA Camp and hike up Manzana Creek Trail. After your walk, proceed west on Figueroa Mountain Road, which traverses a high contour of the mountain and continually reveals wonderful views. Beyond Figueroa Ranger Station, the road drops back down to the Santa Ynez Valley floor.

WINE COUNTRY

Santa Barbara County has a 200-year tradition of grape-growing and winemaking, but only in the last two decades have the Santa Ynez Valley vineyards come of age—as both tourist attractions and producers of excellent wine. Today, about 10,000 acres of grapes supply a couple of dozen vine-yards, most of which offer tasting and tours. The Santa Ynez Valley geography and climate are ideal for wine-producing grapes: The Santa Ynez and San Rafael Mountains are transverse (east-west) ranges, so they channel a cool flow of ocean breezes into the valley. That keeps the prevailing climate temperate, but the valley also has numerous microclimates which allow for plantings of all the classic grape varietals. Whether or not you stop to sample the wines, the country roads that lead to the vineyards are classic backroads through side valleys, canyons, and lovely, open countryside.

To begin a wine tour from where we left off at the intersection of Figueroa Mountain Road and Highway 154, turn left (east) on Highway 154, continue a few miles, then turn

Valleys of grapes framed by chaparral and oak-covered mountains char-acterize much of the Santa Ynez Valley.

right on State Highway 246 toward the towns of Santa Ynez and Solvang.

The first winery you'll come to is the Gainey Vineyard, which has a pretty Spanish-style building, a deli, and a pleasant picnic area. If you see a silent airplane whoosh by overhead, it's a glider from the adjacent airport. At the Gainey Vineyard you can pick up a map of all the Santa Barbara County wineries and fashion, if you wish, your own wine tour. Many of the wineries are quite small, but most offer tasting of some sort. The route I suggest takes in many of the wineries as well as other important sights along the way.

From Gainey, turn left (west) on Highway 246. Pause, if you wish, in the town of Santa Ynez, whose downtown facades have a false-front Old West motif. Turn up Edison Street to Sagunto Street. Here you'll find the Santa Ynez Valley Historical Museum, which depicts life of the Chumash Indians and the early cattle ranchers of the area, and the Parks-Janeway Carriage House, which has a great collection of horse-drawn vehicles.

Back on Highway 246, continue west to Alamo Pintado and turn right (north). Alamo Pintado leads to several small wineries and the valley's smallest community, Ballard. Along the way you'll pass apple orchards and horse farms. Horse breeding is big business in the Santa Ynez Valley, and the farms are kept with the same care that distinguishes the breeding farms of Kentucky—long rows of rail fencing, lovely barns, and handsome animals. Apples are pretty big business, too. In the fall, stands selling apples and cider pop up all over the valley.

Ballard occupies but a few square blocks, so it doesn't take long to see. First, turn right on Baseline Road. You'll see The Ballard Store on the left, but don't try to duck in for a candy bar—this former general store is a gourmet restaurant. When it opened in 1971, it was a true anomaly: French/continental cuisine in an obscure village amid a bunch of horse farms. It seems more at home these days as a natural complement to the wineries and the modern Ballard Inn across the street. Two blocks away (make two

Most Santa Ynez Valley wineries welcome visitors for tasting—here, Carey Cellars on Alamo Pintado Road.

The 1883 Ballard School still serves the tiny community of Ballard.

left turns), the Ballard School, an archetypal little red schoolhouse, is and always has been an elementary school—in operation since 1883.

Back on Alamo Pintado, head north into Los Olivos. This tiny town blends several flavors. It has a fancy inn, some chi-chi galleries, and gingerbread Victorian architecture. It has a wine-tasting room that represents some of the smaller wineries in the valley. The Side Street Cafe is a coffee house that features New Age-tinged symposia and down-home music. My favorite building in town is the Los Olivos Garage, a corrugated-tin gas station where Corvettes and Land Rovers sidle up to the pumps alongside workhorse pickup trucks. Los Olivos may ring a bell for you as home to Michael Jackson and site of Liz Taylor's last wedding, but the local tack shop is much more in keeping with the town's real flavor.

Alamo Pintado leads to Highway 154, where you'll turn left. Immediately on your left is Mattei's Tavern, with its doorway bedecked in lilacs. A frosted glass front window that reads "Santa Barbara Stage Office" indicates the origin of the restaurant/tavern. Swiss Felix Mattei built it in 1886 as a hotel and restaurant to serve stage passengers. Its tavern aspect was fairly clandestine in those days, Mrs. Mattei being a member of the Women's Christian Temperance Union. Mattei's today is elegantly rustic, with intimate dining rooms and historical photos on the walls.

From Mattei's, continue west on Highway 154, then turn right on Foxen Canyon Road, which was once a stage route to Santa Maria. An early, steep rise in the road gives you a fine view of extensive vineyards and the hilltop Firestone Winery, biggest in the Santa Ynez Valley. To visit Firestone, turn left at the intersection with Zaca Station Road. Otherwise, continue right on Foxen Canyon. You'll soon come to one of the newer wineries in the valley, which happens to belong to Davy Crockett/Daniel Boone—aka Fess Parker. The lanky Hollywood hero is a bit of a mogul in Santa Barbara County; he owns an oceanside resort and some cattle ranches, and these days you're likely to find him on duty at his beautifully landscaped winery.

A few miles north you'll come to a right-turn intersection with a dirt road that leads to Zaca Lake. The six-mile jour-

Lilacs frame the entrance to Mattei's Tavern in Los Olivos, originally built as a stagecoach stop, today a popular and atmospheric restaurant.

*Ol' Dan'l Boone himself,
Fess Parker, chats with
wine-tasting visitors to his
Santa Ynez Valley winery.*

ney to the lake is not a quick detour (the road is rough), but
a fine side trip if time permits. Zaca Lake is the rare puddle
in these parts that was not created by a dam. It's a deep,
spring-fed volcanic lake—a great swimming hole and a
wonderful country retreat. A lakeside lodge has a restaurant, 16 cabins, and a campground.

Foxen Canyon road continues north through oak wood-
lands and cattle ranches to another large winery, Zaca
Mesa, and to the more modest Rancho Sisquoc Winery.
High above the intersection with the short road to the win-
ery stands a lonely chapel on a hill—the 1870 San Ramon
Chapel, still in use today.

From here, Foxen Canyon makes a series of 90-degree
bends, presumably around old property lines, and slips
into the tiny town of Sisquoc—a cluster of houses and a
general store. Turn left in Sisquoc on Palmer Road. Tall
fences and oil-drilling machinery are a bit eye-jarring on
this pastoral country road that winds through Cat Canyon
and intersects with Highway 101. After a bucolic reverie in
the Santa Ynez Valley, even this rural stretch of freeway
seems garishly wide and fast.

From here you can go south to Los Alamos and join Tour
3, our other tour of the Santa Ynez Valley, or stay on
Highway 101 to return to Los Angeles.

TOUR 3

Santa Ynez Valley 2: Solvang, Lompoc, and the West Valley

95 miles
Nojoqui Falls County Park • Alisal Ranch • Solvang •
Mission Santa Ines • Los Alamos • La Purisima Mission
• Lompoc • Flower Fields • Jalama Beach • Scenic
Highway 1

The Santa Ynez Valley has so many intriguing backroads that I've divided it into two tours. Tour 2, described in the previous chapter, takes in the valley's thriving wine country and the wild mountain slopes that naturally define its northern boundary. This tour takes in the tourist magnet of Solvang and the colorful flower fields of Lompoc, both familiar, at least by reputation, to many Southern Californians. But we'll also suss out some fairly unknown backroads that are among my favorites in the state.

To begin the tour: Take U.S. Highway 101 north past Santa Barbara and through Gaviota Pass. After you pass through a tunnel, you'll climb a long grade. As you crest the grade,

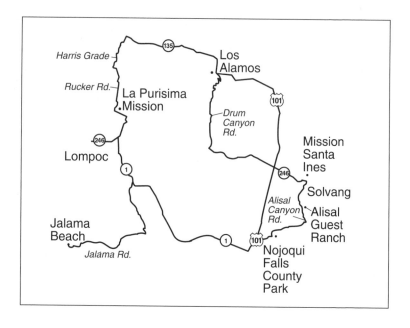

look for a truck parking area on the right. Exit as if you're going to park in this truck parking area, then turn right at the sign that reads "Nojoqui Park."

NOJOQUI FALLS

You'll like the road to Nojoqui Falls. For a brief stretch, it follows the Old Coast Highway, a ghostly remnant of the route mostly erased by Highway 101. This ancient tarmac is overhung by huge, moss-draped oaks—the setting looks creepy at a foggy dusk. Then turn right on Alisal Canyon Road toward Nojoqui Falls County Park. This is a great poppy road in spring when the state flower adds splashes of orange to the green meadows beside the road.

The county park makes a nifty picnic site, but the *raison de visite* is the 10-minute hike to Nojoqui Falls. In summer, the falls may be dry, but it's a pretty walk and a neat sight anyway. Big oaks, sycamores, and bay laurel trees shade the

Poppies and grand oak trees line the winding course of Alisal Road.

path up Nojoqui Creek. In winter and spring, a 160-foot ribbon of water slithers down a mossy face of jalama sandstone and tumbles to a ferny pool at the bottom that looks like a setting where wood nymphs would bathe. Nymphs aside, it's an unusual waterfall because it carries calcium deposits from upstream. Rather than eroding the lip of the cliff, the creek has produced growth at the top of the waterfall, much as stalagmites form in a cave.

Nojoqui Falls slides 160 feet down a mossy face of jalama sandstone.

THE ALISAL

The next several miles of Alisal Canyon Road trace the course of Alisal Creek and pass through thick oak woodland. Spanish moss—lichens, actually—hang from the gnarled limbs of the oaks like a mummy's tattered shroud. The odd cow will appear by the side of the road—an authentic sight on land that has been grazed since early in the nineteenth century when it was part of a huge rancho granted by the Mexican government to Raimundo Carrillo. But after years of prosperity, many years of drought plagued the Mexican rancheros. They broke up the land and sold it to Anglo settlers who were ranchers of a different sort—they recognized reliable ways to augment their cattle income: horses and tourists.

The road finally emerges from the oaks into pasture and comes upon large horse corrals, then the shaded cottages and tended lawns of the Alisal Guest Ranch. It's more luxury resort than dude ranch—although it is a working ranch, and you can take trail rides among 10,000 acres of gorgeous *potrero* landscape. The Alisal has its own spring-fed lake, as well as more traditional resort trappings like a private dining room, golf course, and tennis courts. It's a very civilized country retreat that has drawn Hollywood types since Clark Gable married Lady Silvía in the Alisal library.

SOLVANG

Just north of the ranch, Alisal Road crosses the Santa Ynez River and enters the very different world of Solvang. The preponderance of Danish-themed kitsch can make one a bit cynical about this town, but despite its ersatz trappings, Solvang's Danish identity is authentic.

The name means "sunny vale," and was given to the place by Danish settlers who came here—not from Denmark, but from other Danish settlements in America—

in 1910. The Danes were proud of their heritage, and soon after they platted the township they established Atterdag College—not a college with tests and entry requirements but a center to teach and preserve what the founders considered to be life-enriching Danish traditions. The original site of the college is now the Bit O' Denmark Restaurant, which gives you an idea of the state of things in Solvang today: The town makes no bones about coveting tourist dollars, but gives us a bit of Denmark, and some rich ironies, in the process. So places like this one do serve *frikadeller* (Danish meatballs), *aebelskivers* (ball-shaped pancakes), and Danish open-face sandwiches, but they share the menu with burgers, tostadas, and quiche.

Fortunately, the tradition of Atterdag lives on in the Elverhoy Museum, and I heartily encourage every Solvang visitor to seek it out as a wonderful refuge from Solvang's unabashed commercialism. As you come into town on Alisal Road, turn left on Elverhoy Way. The gingerbread house that contains the museum was handbuilt by artist Viggo Brandt-Erichsen in the late 1940s in a style derived from eighteenth-century farmhouses in Jutland, northern Denmark. The museum is devoted to Danish culture and Solvang history. Individual rooms are decorated and furnished to represent Danish styles—a farm kitchen with handpainted flowers on the walls and cupboards, a spinning room, and the "best room," or parlor, so called because it was maintained at its best for special visitors and occasions. Lots of old photographs show the early days of Solvang. It seems that the community floundered for awhile, and it took intensive promotion among Danes in Nebraska and Iowa to get more settlers in and to secure its future. Elverhoy is a charming museum that has the feeling of a warm and welcoming home.

Solvang's future was really secured in 1946, when the *Saturday Evening Post* published an article about the town's

Solvang is rife with Danish kitsch, but its Scandinavian roots are genuine and the cuisine often authentic.

Danish character, and tourists began to arrive to check it out. Today it's a melange of gift shops, Danish restaurants, Danish bakeries, and a lot of other businesses, such as outlet shops and decidedly un-Danish restaurants, happy to cash in on the flow of tourists. One of its prime attractions is the outdoor theater of the Pacific Conservatory for the Performing Arts (PCPA). Plays presented during the summer Theaterfest place professionals on stage with students in classical and modern performances.

MISSION SANTA INES

Ironically, Solvang's most noteworthy landmark has no Danish pretensions at all. The Spanish Mission Santa Ines happens to fall into Solvang city limits on the east edge of town. (The mission is usually spelled by the proper Spanish spelling, "Ines." But because the Spanish used to capriciously interchange I's and Y's, Z's and S's, the town and the river eventually assumed the spelling "Ynez.") The first mission church was built in 1804 and was destroyed by an earthquake in 1812. The present structure was completed in

1817. The mission of the missions was, of course, to convert Indians to Christianity. But in the process, the Indians were kept in virtual slavery, and it was here in 1824 that the natives revolted against their saviors. They attacked Spanish soldiers at the mission and burned a number of the buildings, then retreated to La Purisima Mission (in Lompoc), where they were finally subdued. Santa Ines, like all the missions, was secularized in the 1830s by the Mexican government and fell into decay. The current mission has been beautifully restored, with adobe walls six feet thick supporting huge, hand-hewn beams. .

SPLIT-PEA CITY

When you're pleasantly stuffed with pastries or aebelskivers, head north on Alisal Road to State Highway 246 and turn left (west). A few miles along and across Highway 101, you'll come to a sight familiar to freeway travelers: Pea Soup Andersen's. Freeway billboards all up and down Highway 101 guide hungry travelers to Andersen's. The Andersen family has been serving pea soup on this site since 1924, when Anton Andersen and his wife Juliette opened a little roadside cafe. They called it Andersen's Electrical Cafe in honor of their newfangled electric range, but later changed the name as Juliette's specialty gained statewide renown.

The cartoon characters featured on the ubiquitous billboards first appeared in *Judge* magazine in the 1940s. It showed two men in an industrial setting, splitting peas with a hammer and chisel, and was captioned "Little-known occupations." The Andersens received permission to use the characters, and in 1946 held a big contest to name them. For the record, they're called Hap-Pea and Pea-Wee. You can pose out front of the restaurant with your face filling a cutout of Hap-Pea or Pea-Wee, which I think is a very worthwhile thing to do. So is eating there. I recommend the

Traveler's Special: $4.95 gets you all the pea soup you can eat (drink?), bread and butter, and a beverage. I've heard the record is 17 bowls in one sitting, but I think I topped that once after subsisting for a few days on freeze-dried glop while backpacking in the San Rafael Wilderness. Laugh if you will at Pea Soup Andersen's hokiness. I like the place.

REMEMBER LOS ALAMOS

Continue west on Highway 246 toward Lompoc. We'll visit the Valley of Flowers soon, but first, we must turn right (north) on Drum Canyon Road (just after you cross Santa Rosa Creek) toward Los Alamos. This is another great country road. It starts out in a broad, cultivated valley that narrows to a long meadow, freckled with wildflowers. Wild mustard outlines the road like nature's hi-lite marker. Lane stripes soon fade away as this seemingly forgotten road climbs and winds over the Purisima Hills. It feels like no one's been here in years. The road then crests the range and descends past a cemetery and a park and into the heart of downtown Los Alamos.

Such as it is, Los Alamos doesn't seem to have changed much since it was a stage stop in the 1880s. It's fitting that antiques are its main attraction. Kroll's is the largest of the antique shops you'll find along Bell Street, the town's short main drag. A sign inside the warehouse-like building proclaims, "This is not a museum, all this junk is 4 sale." Museum or junk, it's a great place to browse, especially among the Coca Cola machines and a great collection of old road signs.

Kroll's is at the east end of Bell Street. At the other end of town is the weatherbeaten facade of the Union Hotel. The hotel was built in 1880 to serve stage passengers and has been lovingly restored with period furnishings. Today it's a weekend bed-and-breakfast inn, a restaurant that serves family-style meals of prodigious portions, and a saloon with swinging doors, just like in the westerns. The hotel is full of the whimsy of its late owner/restorer, Dick Langdon. The ceiling of the saloon is made up of an old lettered store-front—"The People's Store"—and the hombres' room floor is made up of old state license plates.

But this is nothing compared to what Langdon created next door in the Victorian Mansion. To say that this six-room hotel has theme rooms is a gross understatement. They're more like fantasy rooms, ingeniously created to provide an escape from the outside world. In the '50s Drive-In room you sleep in the back of a pink Cadillac (really!) from which you can watch movies like *Rebel Without a Cause* on a 10-foot screen. In the Gypsy Room you sleep in a gypsy wagon to the sound of croaking frogs and babbling water, and watch movies like *King of the Gypsies*. Every room has a hidden bathroom door, but they'll show you where it is if you insist. Appropriate costume bathrobes are provided, and breakfast appears magically in your own private food compartment.

The Victorian Mansion annex to the Union Hotel in Los Alamos is a six-room fantasy retreat from the real world.

In the 1950s Drive-In Movie Room of the Victorian Mansion, guests sleep in the back of a Cadillac and watch classic movies on a 10-foot screen.

There's not a single light switch in the place—everything, including the TV, VCR, stereo, hot tub, and lights, is wired to operate by a single remote control. It's all ridiculous and irresistible. Either way, you have to see it to believe it.

La Purisima

Leave Los Alamos by heading west on Bell Street and west on State Highway 135 through the Los Alamos Valley farmland and vineyards. Turn left at the sign that steers you to Lompoc. This road is called Harris Grade, and it leads over a higher section of the Purisima Hills than does Drum Canyon. It tops out in a scruffy pine forest and reveals a view of the many red-tile roofs of Lompoc. At the bottom of the grade, bear left on Rucker Road, then left and left again into La Purisima Mission State Historic Park.

La Purisima is the rare mission that is not a parish church, so I always feel a bit less intrusive tromping around here than at others. It's also the most fully restored mission and, surrounded by state parkland, has the most authentic setting. (Fourteen miles of trails wander through the Burton Mesa chaparral that surrounds the mission.) All the buildings have been rebuilt and furnished 1820s-style; even the original aqueduct and pond system are maintained. (Much of the restoration work was done during the Depression by the Civilian Conservation Corps. The CCC molded 110,000 adobe bricks and hand-made 32,000 tiles.) Livestock on the grounds add an authentic touch. The only thing missing at La Purisima is conscripted Indians.

La Purisima was plagued from the outset by earthquakes and floods, and later by the Indian revolt of 1824. The revolt that began at Mission Santa Ines ended here, with several deaths among the Indians and Spanish soldiers. Mike Marinacci's book *Mysterious California* reports a lot of strange goings-on at La Purisima—skeletons of smallpox-stricken infants under the tile chapel floor, a ghostly gardener who tends the grounds, and a ghost in the kitchen. My favorite story has to do with the tomb of the longtime mission pastor, Fray Mariano Payeras. When his tomb was exhumed many years ago, the lower half of the padre's body was missing. His waist and legs turned up at Mission Santa Barbara, but no one knows why he was bisected and given separate burials.

LOMPOC AND THE FLOWERS

From the mission, follow the connector road to Highway 246 and turn west toward Lompoc. The highway becomes Ocean Avenue, the main drag through Lompoc's old downtown. A number of the old buildings here are painted with murals depicting Lompoc scenes and history, most of them along Ocean Avenue and H Street. My favorite one (at 137 South H Street) is a strange sight—a gang of women appear to be playing tug-of-war with a building. It seems that Lompoc was founded in 1874 as a temperance colony, but the

WCTU ladies had a terrible time fending off demon rum. In 1884, a vigilante committee wound a strong rope around a local den of iniquity, yanked it off its foundation, and dragged it for a block, spilling booze into the streets of Lompoc.

Lompoc is called the Valley of Flowers not for the wildflowers, which certainly are abundant on the hillsides, but for the cultivated flower fields that supply at least half of the world's flower seeds. More than 1,000 acres of flowers and more than 30 varieties grow in and around Lompoc from early June through August. You'll have no trouble spotting flower fields during that time—many are along Purisima Road near the mission, off Highway 246 on Sweeny and Santa Rosa roads, and along Ocean Avenue as you come into town. The Chamber of Commerce at 111 South I Street can give you an up-to-the-minute map of what is in bloom where. For a bird's-eye view of the Valley of Flowers, drive up to the Observation Point—signs will lead you there from Ocean Avenue. During Lompoc's annual Flower Festival, held the last weekend of June, narrated tours take you to a number of flower fields and explain the flower seed industry.

JALAMA BEACH

Jalama Beach, 15 miles southwest of Lompoc, is one of Southern California's great secrets. Maybe it's because Jalama is not a storybook California beach nor a place for casual swimmers or sun worshippers. Jalama is wild and isolated, requiring 15 miles of hilly, winding road to get there, and an affinity for cold, rough surf, chilly fog, and strong winds to stick around. It's fabled among surfers and windsurfers, but anyone who enjoys fresh, bracing air and quiet isolation will love Jalama.

To get there, take Highway 1 south from Lompoc and turn right on Jalama Road. Except for one or two ranch driveways along the way, the road is uninterrupted as it winds around

Jalama Road emerges from a mountain crossing at a wild, unsettled stretch of Jalama Beach.

deep wooded canyons and over hills of wild oats. The last couple of miles are through low, windswept chaparral. Finally, the road makes a sharp bend, crosses railroad tracks (in spring, look for giant yellow coreopsis flowers along the road), and emerges upon a grand ocean view of beaches and cliffs extending for many undeveloped miles northward. Most of the coastline in this vista is part of Vandenberg Air Force Base and is off-limits, but the view is all yours.

Jalama has a campground, picnic area, and lots of wide-open beach for combing, walking, and reflecting—perhaps upon how all of Southern California's beaches were once like this.

After your stay at Jalama, you'll have to backtrack on Jalama Road to Highway 1. Turn right and follow it through the rugged Santa Ynez Mountains until it joins Highway 101 just a few miles south of Nojoqui Pass where this tour began.

TOUR 4

e Santa Monica Mountains

87 miles
*Topanga Canyon • Mulholland Highway • Malibu Creek
State Park • Paramount Ranch • Peter Strauss Ranch •
Decker Canyon • Little Sycamore Canyon Road •
Sandstone Peak • Circle X Ranch • County Line Beach •
Point Mugu State Park • Malibu*

The Santa Monica Mountains are a modern miracle. In plain view of urban skyscrapers and endless suburban sprawl, you can walk a trail and see a bobcat or coyote slither across your path. You can drive roads that feel remote from anything remotely civilized, then stop for a soda at a country store or a steak at a country restaurant. You can see vestiges of the Old West. You can drive so close to the ocean your windshield might receive a spritzing of saltwater, yet you're never more than 30 to 45 minutes away from Los Angeles. And despite the crushing pressures of development, population, and pollution, the Santa Monicas feel like a rugged island.

The Santa Monicas are one of the west-east transverse ranges of Southern California. The mountain chain rises out of the level farming plains of Oxnard, follows the coast for about 30 miles, then runs another 15 miles through the heart of the city to Griffith Park. Average width is about 10 miles.

The rugged mountains represent a number of geological epochs. For much of its history, the land was under a shallow sea, accounting for an abundance of exposed sandstone. But while the sedimentary rock was forming, the mountains entered a volcanic period. And more recently, compressive forces have been working to uplift the mountains, buckling and fracturing the layers of rock. So the Santa Monicas, while not particularly high (tallest point is 3,111 feet), are young and rugged. The canyon walls are steep, and many exposed peaks are extremely sheer. But streams tumble down many of the ravines, meadows open up among the dense chaparral and oak woodlands, and the Pacific laps at the southern edge of the range, making for a great variety of scenery easily visible from a network of backroads—many of them astoundingly rural considering the urban proximity of the mountains.

Fortunately for visitors, many of the prime parcels of the Santa Monicas are public land. Within the 70,000-acre Santa Monica Mountains National Recreation Area, a flotilla of agencies administers a patchwork quilt of parks: the National Park Service, Los Angeles County, California State Parks, and the Santa Monica Mountains Conservancy, among others.

Our focus will be on the coastal stretch of the Santa Monicas, which is laced with north-south canyon roads and one long, sinuous, east-west road that follows the spine of the mountains much of the way before it plays out at the Pacific Ocean.

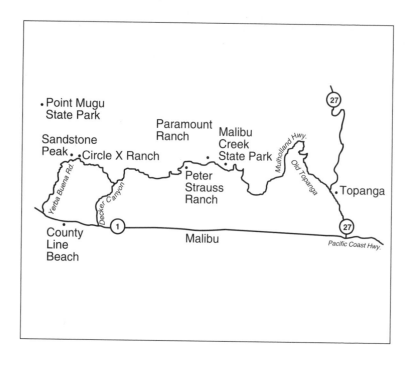

To begin the tour: Take the Santa Monica Freeway (Interstate 10) west to Pacific Coast Highway. Continue west on Pacific Coast Highway about 10 miles to Topanga Canyon Boulevard and turn right.

TOPANGA CANYON TO SADDLE PEAK LODGE

Topanga Canyon Boulevard winds into the mountains along Topanga Creek through thick coastal chaparral—the tangle of manzanita, chamise, sage, toyon, scrub oak, and other shrubs that make up what is sometimes called elfin forest, the dominant vegetation throughout the Santa Monicas. Chaparral requires periodic fire to propagate itself. But when it doesn't burn for long periods of time, the undergrowth builds up and a chaparral fire becomes an uncontrollable conflagration. That's what happened in November 1993, when a fire that started on the other side of the range in Calabasas burned through here and other Santa Monica Mountain canyons. You'll see evidence of this and other chaparral fires in various places on this tour.

Topanga Canyon Boulevard squeezes through a dramatic portal of sheer cliffs just before it crests in the town of Topanga. An odd mix of folk live in the Santa Monicas, and they all seem to convene in Topanga. New agers, leftover hippies, yuppies in Jeeps, and rednecks all coexist and find commerce that caters to them. "Downtown" Topanga has a couple of boutiques, country markets, casual restaurants, a health food store, and an establishment that's as much a spiritual experience as a restaurant. The Inn of the Seventh Ray is romantically perched on the banks of the creek, exuding a lot of peace and love and high cosmic vibrations . . . and good food, too.

Turn left on Old Topanga Road (the Inn of the Seventh Ray is on the corner), which continues along the winding course of Topanga Creek through the oak-shaded heart of Old Topanga. After a series of switchbacks reach a high saddle, the road dips down to intersect Mulholland Highway. Road cuts along this downhill stretch of Old Topanga expose layers of ancient sediments and are popular fossil-gathering spots.

Turn left on Mulholland Highway and pass some of those so-called "country living" communities that huddle behind imposing gates. Continue several miles to Cold Canyon Road—actually the *third* Cold Canyon Road on the left. Cold Canyon is a quiet side road that descends into a neighborhood of old, authentic "country living" homes, and meets Piuma Road. Just at that intersection of country roads is a hidden gem of a restaurant, Saddle Peak Lodge. Dining here is like dining in an old hunting lodge, replete with log walls, mounted trophy heads, and a big stone fireplace. The cuisine is meaty and, well, not cheap. High above the lodge is

Saddle Peak, the highest in this part of the mountains, nicely dressed in a variety of antennae and dishes.

MALIBU CREEK STATE PARK

Turn right on Piuma Road and right again on Malibu Canyon Road, and you'll quickly come to Malibu Creek State Park. If you feel like stretching your legs, this is a good place to do it. Easy walking trails parallel the creek, pass beneath massive valley oaks, and lead to little Century Lake, surrounded by reeds, favored by birds, and croaking with Pacific tree frogs late in the day. Does some of the scenery seem familiar? The craggy volcanic formation west of the lake, Goat Buttes, was seen in the opening sequence of the *M*A*S*H* television series. In fact, Malibu Creek stood in as Korea for all the series' outdoor sequences. The site of the old set is about a half-mile beyond the lake. The park has a real Hollywood pedigree: It also stood in as paradise in some Tarzan movies, as Wales in *How Green Was My Valley*, and as an alien planet in *Planet of the Apes*. Much of the land was once owned by Bob Hope and Ronald Reagan.

This setting may look familiar to fans of the old M*A*S*H *television series. Exteriors were filmed here in Malibu Creek State Park.*

S
M
by ....on in Malibu
Creek State Park.

Back in the car, turn left on Malibu Canyon Road and immediately left again on Mulholland. For the next several miles, you'll be paralleling Malibu Creek, looking down on a valley that was once part of the Reagan Ranch. The oddly shaped peaks on the opposite side of the valley show the tilting and uplifting of the compressive forces working on the range. At the intersection with Cornell Road, turn right and into Paramount Ranch.

PARAMOUNT RANCH

Remember I mentioned vestiges of the Old West? Well, here they are, Hollywood style. Paramount Pictures once owned 4,000 acres of these rolling hills and valleys and used them for numerous westerns and other movies from the '20s through the '40s. The 1937 film *The Adventures of Marco Polo* brought elephants, 2,000 horses and a huge fortress to the ranch. In the 1950s, Paramount Ranch was home to TV westerns like *Bat Masterson* and *Have Gun Will Travel*. The old western mining town you see on the property today was actually cobbled together from old Twentieth Century Fox sets, some years after Paramount sold the property. Most recently, the village has served as the exterior setting for the television show *Dr. Quinn, Medicine Woman*.

OLD CORNELL

Return to Mulholland and continue west. Just below you to the left is Malibu Lake, a pretty, "look-but-don't-touch" lake (created by a dam across Malibu Creek) surrounded by private homes. Soon you come into an oak-shaded valley.

Privileged residents of Malibu Lake enjoy a serene setting in the midst of the rugged mountains.

On your right is a great country eatery called, simply, The Old Place. It looks like an abandoned shack (it was actually the post office for Cornell, a village that has pretty much disappeared from modern maps), but the place is hopping on weekends. The menu consists of exactly two items, steak

The Old Place on Mulholland Highway is the old Cornell Post Office building. The country eatery has exactly two items on the menu: clams and steak.

and clams. The clams are always fresh, and if they run out, well, you know what's for dinner. Directly opposite The Old Place is Peter Strauss Ranch (former home of the actor), and Lake Enchanto, a small park with picnicking beneath some magnificent oak trees.

There's yet another popular country joint just down the road. You can't miss The Rock Store—it's the place with the antique gas pumps and a few dozen large motorcycles out front. Once the general store for Cornell, The Rock Store is now a weekend biker hangout that serves up barbecued tri-tip, chicken, and burgers.

HIGH MULHOLLAND

Beyond The Rock Store, Mulholland begins switchbacking out of the valley to a spectacular overlook from which you can see much of the valley-and-ridge landscape you've been driving, as well as the Santa Susana and even the San Gabriel Mountains to the northeast.

Mulholland follows a higher course for awhile now. Across Kanan-Dume Road is another day-use park, Rocky Oaks, that in wet years has a wonderful pond full of lasciviously croaking frogs. Just about across the street is Calamigos Ranch, a more upscale country-style barbecue restaurant. From here Mulholland wanders along a high

This country chapel is among the Old West movie sets of Paramount Ranch in the Santa Monica Mountains National Recreation Area. Westerns and television programs are frequently filmed here, but the property is also open to the public.

View of serpentine Mulholland Highway (foreground), the only major east-west route across the Santa Monica Mountains.

ridge of the Santa Monicas. Eerie spires of red volcanic rock seem to stare down upon the road like hungry vultures. To the south, you can peer down the long V of a canyon that forms a gunsight frame, at the end of which is the Pacific Ocean and Santa Catalina Island. After tracing this high ridge for a few miles, Mulholland joins Decker Canyon Road (State Highway 23). Turn left.

Decker Canyon follows another high ridge via a series of hairpin turns—definitely not standard-issue state highway material. Decker has that narrow, meandering aspect of European country roads, but the designer horse farms along the way are uniquely Californian. A few miles south, Mulholland leaves Decker Canyon by way of a right turn.

TO BONEY RIDGE

Now, from here you could follow Mulholland all the way down to the ocean—a really wonderful drive. But that's the obvious route. Instead, almost immediately after you make the right on Mulholland, turn right again on Little

Sycamore Canyon Road. But for a few striking country homes, you feel all alone in this, the highest part of the Santa Monicas. This is a great road. It snakes and dips and sharply bends along another high ridge, with alternating views: south, over a series of hilltops to the ocean; north, across the Conejo Valley to the Topa Topa Mountains. In front of you, like a giant stegosaurus spine, is Boney Ridge, the crest of the Santa Monicas, and Sandstone Peak, at 3,111 feet, the highest point in the range. Sandstone is mis-named—the rock formations of the ridge and peak are volcanic in origin. At the base of the mountain, you'll see a small dirt parking lot and a sign for the Backbone Trail. This trail, which one day will extend 65 miles across the entire Santa Monica range, leads to the summit of Sandstone Peak. It's not a difficult hike, and the view is magnificent.

As the road descends, you'll come to headquarters for Circle X Ranch, an old Boy Scout camp now in the hands of the National Park Service, which has a fine, oak-shaded campground and picnic area.

Our road has changed names to Yerba Buena now, and begins a long descent through Little Sycamore Canyon to the ocean. At the foot of Yerba Buena, just to the left, is County Line Beach, a popular surfing and windsurfing spot and site of a funky hangout called Neptune's Net. The surf crowd, cruising bikers, and sundry passers-by all wander into the Net for fresh shellfish, fish and chips, drinks, to survey the waves, and to hang.

On the Beach

Turn right now on Pacific Coast Highway (PCH) to enjoy one of the most dramatic stretches of coastal road this side of Big Sur. From County Line to Point Mugu, PCH hugs the shoreline along a corridor blasted from rocky mountains that would otherwise tumble directly into the surf. The roadbuilding effort required displacing 2.5 million cubic

Pacific Coast Highway skirts a narrow shelf between mountain and ocean where the Santa Monica Mountains dip into the sea at Point Mugu.

yards of mountainside. South of Sycamore Canyon, crews blasted through a full mile of solid rock cliff and dumped the ensuing tens of thousands of cubic yards of riprap into the sea to control erosion. It took nearly a decade to complete (1921–29), a lot of explosives, and a lot of human daring. The original road skirted the ocean side of Point Mugu. In the late 1930s, road crews cleaved the promontory to put in the wider road as it is today.

Along this stretch of road are coastal and mountain parklands, all part of Point Mugu State Park. Big Sycamore Canyon is one of the prettiest, gentlest canyons in the mountains. You can park at the campground and take a wonderful stroll along a stream shaded by coast live oaks and broadleaf sycamore trees. Across the highway is a sandy pocket beach, and just up the road is a giant sand dune on the inland side (a sure hit with kids) and, along La Jolla Beach, some rare, right-on-the-beach camping. At the upper end of this beach, a trail leads through the mountains to La Jolla Valley, which contains one of California's best preserved remnants of native bunchgrass prairie.

If you drive PCH in March, your eye will be distracted to the mountain side of the road by the presence of giant coreopsis wildflowers—huge, ostentatious green stalks and yellow blossoms that erupt right out of the rocky cliffs.

Point Mugu is a natural turn-back spot for this tour. You can park right at the point or just beyond it and savor a fine view of the ocean, the waves, the gulls circling, and the pelicans fishing. Above the point, the landscape changes considerably. On the coast side of the highway you can see Mugu Lagoon, a 900-acre salt marsh that draws tens of thousands of migratory birds. You can only enjoy it from afar, though, as the lagoon lies within the U.S. Navy's Pacific Missile Test Center. Inland, the Santa Monica Mountains give way to the fertile fields of the Oxnard Plain.

After you turn back and pass County Line Beach once again, PCH ceases to be anything like a backroad. You're in Malibu now, and the highway becomes four-lane and fast but still offers some fine ocean and mountain views. You'll also see some of the amazing homes for which Malibu is so famous—*Architectural Digest* fantasies tucked against the mountainsides and lording over the long strands of sand.

But you don't have to show a SAG (Screen Actor's Guild) card to enjoy the beach in Malibu. "Coastal Access" signs point the way to numerous public access spots, perhaps to the chagrin of the privileged. But they have their dream homes. The beach is ours. The best, uncrowded beaches are four that lie in succession at the base of tall cliffs: Nicholas Canyon, El Pescador, La Piedra, and El Matador.

In the congested heart of Malibu is the romantic Malibu Pier and Alice's Restaurant. It's not Arlo Guthrie's Alice's, but an excellent restaurant that overlooks Surfrider Beach—site of all those *Beach Blanket Bingo/Gidget*-type movies.

Below the commercial core of Malibu, the highway forms a corridor between beachfront homes and steep hillsides, all of which burned in the November 1993 fire. Just past

Topanga Canyon Boulevard, where this mountain/beach tour began, is the opulent J. Paul Getty Museum. You can't just drop in on J. Paul—he wants a call in advance (310-459-8402). But the museum, a replica of a seaside villa buried by the eruption of Mount Vesuvius, is a stunning place with an almost unimaginably rich endowment, housing everything from priceless antiquities to priceless Impressionists.

From the Getty, it's just a few miles down-coast to Santa Monica and the Santa Monica Freeway.

TOUR 5

The San Gabriel Mountains

123 miles
La Cañada Flintridge • Angeles Crest Highway • Mount Wilson • Big Pines • Wrightwood • Devil's Punchbowl • Upper Big Tujunga Canyon • Angeles Forest Highway • Hidden Springs • Big Tujunga River

The San Gabriels are "our" mountains, as much a part of the Southern California signature as the beaches or the downtown skyline. These are the mountains that hover in crisp outline above the Rose Bowl and help convince millions of football and parade viewers that Southern California must be paradise on earth.

Of course, the minions don't suffer through the days when smog so shrouds the cuff of the range that its peaks are invisible from below. But to locals, that's all the more reason to rejoice in the fortuitous proximity of the San Gabriel Mountains and the Angeles National Forest which contains most of the mountain range. Despite the airborne indignities launched at the mountains, despite the creep of development up every unprotected foothill, the San Gabriels remain a genuine, if beleaguered, refuge. It takes only a few uphill bends of the Angeles Crest Highway to

49

feel welcome in a wild place where the air is cool and clean,
pine trees stand tall, and clear streams tumble through
rugged chaparral canyons.

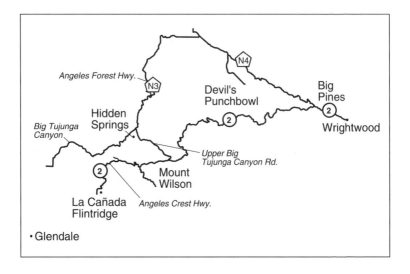

To begin the tour: Take State Highway 2, the Glendale
Freeway, north from Glendale. After a jog to the east in the
foothills, Highway 2 becomes the Angeles Crest Highway.
Proceed north.

ANGELES CREST HIGHWAY

The Angeles Crest is a wondrous work of mountain-road
engineering as it snakes its way across the spine of the San
Gabriels. It has all the grandeur of the most dramatic mountain highways—road cuts chiseled from solid rock walls,
great sweeping vistas, high canyon bridges—but it's not one
of those hairpin-turn routes with barely room for two oncom-
ing cars. No, the Angeles Crest was built Los Angeles-style:
wide and fast. It took nearly 30 years (1929–56) of work by

The sinuous Angeles Crest Highway slides through the front range of the San Gabriel Mountains, here just a few miles above La Cañada Flintridge.

Depression-era laborers, inmates, and road crews to complete the 55 miles of highway from La Cañada Flintridge ("a town so nice they named it twice") to Wrightwood.

The road climbs steadily and leaves the foothill community quickly. If you give it notice, you can't help but marvel at the construction effort required to build it, for these are steep mountains. Williamson Bridge spans a sheer chasm, and all sorts of run-off channels and stabilizing devices keep the road from tumbling down into the deep Arroyo Seco.

The high quality of the Angeles Crest Highway also contributes to its danger. A lot of urban hotshots use it as a speedway. I much prefer the pace of a weekday, but numerous turnouts allow you to pull over and let the speed demons go. Even on weekends, traffic thins out past Red Box Ranger Station. Weather is often a concern in these mountains: Dry summer and fall months bring fire danger; wet winters bring snow to the higher elevations and heavy rains and occasional slides to the lower slopes. Always carry chains in winter, even when the road is plowed.

Although the peaks ahead portend a beautiful mountain drive, sign pollution plagues the beginning of the highway. The Forest Service, intent on its bureaucratic duty, doesn't see the irony of the visual pollution it wreaks by slapping up at least a dozen placards, including the obvious "National Forests Need Their Trees" and the ominous "You Are Required to Know Forest Regulations." (Will there be a quiz at Red Box Station?) Another sign informs you that this is a National Forest Scenic Byway, so the Angeles Crest has the dual honor of being both a state and federal scenic highway.

For the first 15 miles, the Angeles Crest follows a high contour above the Arroyo Seco, the deep canyon that carves an arc on your right as you climb—first north, then east into the heart of the mountains. After 10 miles you'll come to the Clear Creek Information Center, which is usually open on weekends to dispense maps and up-to-date information. It's a good idea to find out what might be closed in the forest; fire danger and budget cuts occasionally force the closure of dirt roads, picnic areas, and campgrounds.

SWITZER'S

Just beyond Clear Creek you'll come to a parking area for Switzer's. There's a story behind most names in the San Gabriels, and Switzer is prominent among them. Perry Switzer established a wilderness camp here in 1884. He was called "Commodore" Switzer for his "fleet" of burros that brought visitors up the rugged trail to the camp beside a waterfall in the misnamed Arroyo Seco ("dry gully"). Like most mountain resorts in the San Gabriels, Switzer's had a checkered history of fire and flood. It burned in 1896, was resurrected in 1905, and was transformed in 1912 by Lloyd and Bertha Austin into a popular resort called Switzer-Land. Hundreds of weekend visitors would make the trip by stagecoach and burro to hike, fish, or laze about in a hammock. In 1924, the Austins built a stunning stone chapel perched above the Switzer Falls. The resort was pretty much wiped out by a flood in March 1938. By then, the Angeles Crest was already paved beyond Switzer's, and the novelty of the place had worn off. The Forest Service razed the chapel and other remaining buildings in the '40s and '50s, but a walk-in picnic area (a half-mile) and a trail down to the falls (another mile) remain as homage to those early years of visitation to the San Gabriels.

RED BOX

After Switzer's, the road bends east and arrives at the intersection with Mount Wilson Road at Red Box Ranger Station. Red Box (named for a box of firefighting equipment outside the station) is a saddle between the Arroyo Seco and the West Fork of the San Gabriel River. If Clear Creek is closed, Red Box is more likely to be open for maps and information. Remember, in this era of budget cuts, anything can be closed at any time. One closure that appears permanent is the road down to the West Fork. It's a hike now, four miles to the river and another mile to a trail camp, but the reward is a sylvan setting: a permanent stream shaded by alder, oak, maple, and spruce trees. Red Box is also the trailhead for a hike to Strawberry Peak, highest in the front range of the San Gabriels (6,164 feet).

MOUNT WILSON

If the Angeles Crest Highway is an amazing feat of construction, the road to Mount Wilson is dazzling. Whittled almost entirely out of solid rock, the four-mile paved road clings to the edge of a cluster of minor peaks until it reaches the broad, wooded summit of Mount Wilson, 5,710 feet.

The first thing you notice atop Mount Wilson is the cluster of antennae, dishes, and erector-set gizmos that adorn its crest. The summit is the nexus for much of Los Angeles's television and radio transmission. The old Mount Wilson Hotel, torn down in the 1960s, used to proudly claim that "Mount Wilson is the television and FM transmitter capital of the world." As you drive around these high-tech eyesores toward the parking lot, you'll skirt the city side of the mountain, where the view may be stunning, nondescript, or nauseating, depending on the level of pollution.

Ironically, the very conditions that create the basin's smog-trapping inversion layer make Mount Wilson an excellent site for viewing the heavens, despite the sea of city lights below. The top of the mountain is just above the inversion layer, an obvious fact when you look out over the sea of smog or fog just below. (Don't worry, there are lots of clear days, too.) This creates placid atmospheric conditions, devoid of aerial turbulence that blurs the viewing from inland observatories. This was a fact understood by Dr. George Ellery Hale as early as 1903. Hale obtained a grant from the Carnegie Institution to build first a 60-inch, then a 100-inch telescope atop Mount Wilson. The toll road (a dirt path) up the south side of the mountain had to be widened and a special gasoline/electric truck had to be built to transport the heavy parts of the telescope. The 100-inch telescope was the largest in the world when completed in 1917 and remained so until the 200-inch Hale Telescope was built atop Mount Palomar (see Tour 9).

The Mount Wilson telescopes are still scientifically important, and the atmosphere is still ideal for stellar viewing. City lights do preclude exploration of the most distant galaxies, but the telescopes are used to study stars within our own galaxy. One ongoing project is the search for planets (and possibly, life) around 100 nearby stars. Two solar observatories (the tall towers) are also part of the Mount Wilson complex. At this writing, tours were being offered from April through October at 1 p.m. on weekends. The tour begins in the pavilion of Skyline Park, the Forest Service picnic area, between the communications antennae and the observatory.

ANGELES HIGH COUNTRY

The Angeles Crest beyond Red Box begins to feel more remote. Traffic thins out (unless it's a prime day for skiing), and it's just a great mountain drive for many miles, with turnouts and picnic areas along the way and trails leading into canyons and up the high backcountry peaks. (Hikers should obtain a copy of John W. Robinson's *Trails of the Angeles*, the bible of backcountry exploration in the San Gabriels.) The view to the right (south) is of the wild West Fork country and the San Gabriel Wilderness. If you're camping, Chilao is a nice campground, and if you need refreshing, Newcomb's store/cafe is the only grub stop until Wrightwood. The road climbs almost imperceptibly until it reaches Cloudburst Summit, 7,108 feet, and the Mount Waterman Ski Area, the oldest ski area in the San Gabriels and the closest to the metropolis.

As the road continues along a high ridge, with views to the north extending down to the Antelope Valley of the Mojave Desert, it passes Kratka Ridge Ski Area then offers a dramatic view south into Bear Canyon. A closed dirt road carves a squiggly line in the steep mountainside: It once connected the Angeles Crest with State Highway 39 and the Crystal Lake Recreation Area. A sign here warns of the possible presence of bighorn sheep, most likely to be seen on the steep rock faces between the two highway tunnels that lance Mount Williamson.

This next stretch of road is occasionally closed in winter, and snow lingers in shady side canyons well into summer. Dawson Saddle, 7,901 feet, is the highest point on the Angeles Crest and offers the most stunning view of the Mojave Desert. The road then cuts across Vincent Gap, where there's a big parking area, rest rooms, and trailheads. You can descend on foot three miles into Vincent Gap and the East Fork of the San Gabriel River or make the climb to the top of Mount Baden-Powell, the dominant peak in these parts, named for the founder of the Boy Scouts. Gnarled old limber pines on Mount Baden-Powell are believed to be 1,000 to 2,000 years old. Or you can just stop to enjoy the view, which takes in the East Fork country and the 10,064-foot summit of Mount San Antonio, better known as Old Baldy, the highest peak in the San Gabriels. Or look the other way, toward the desert, and see an obvious section of the San Andreas Fault.

BIG PINES AND WRIGHTWOOD

From Vincent Gap, the highway climbs to Blue Ridge Summit, then drops down to Big Pines, site of a fine old ranger station beside which is a distinctive stone tower. The tower once had a twin, and a big sign stretched between them to welcome visitors to Big Pines Recreation Area. The sister tower was razed to allow widening of the highway. Poetry lovers will surely want to pause to read the verse of one William A. Bristol, whose flowery sentiments are immortalized on a bronze plaque on the tower, dated 1925:

"There is music in the forest in the pines
And its murmur ever swells and declines
And the trees though old and hoary
Sing a sweet aeolian story
To the soul that for their glory
E'er repines."

He wrote two more verses, but I'll spare you.

Near Big Pines are two ski areas: Sunrise to the north and Mountain High to the east. Mountain High is also a summer mountain bike center. Officially, our tour reverses direction here. But if you're in need of services, continue descending through the Swarthout Valley, which happens to be the exact course of the San Andreas Fault, into Wrightwood.

Wrightwood is a pleasant, pine-shaded town with motels, cabin rentals, and places to eat. Turn up Park Drive to enter the heart of the village. The drive is lined with cafes, antique shops, and galleries.

A Choice of Return Routes: At this point I offer two suggestions for returning to the Los Angeles Area. Both routes eventually join on the Angeles Forest Highway and slice the mountains through the spectacular Tujunga Narrows. The longer return dips down to the high-desert Antelope Valley and visits the bizarre geological site known as Devil's Punchbowl. Or, if you're strictly in a mountain mood, reverse direction on Highway 2, the Angeles Crest Highway. Shortly past Charlton Flat, turn down Upper Big Tujunga Canyon Road.

RETURN VIA DEVIL'S PUNCHBOWL

If you're an earthquake buff, by all means choose this route. When you stand at Big Pines Visitor Center, you're athwart the highest point on the San Andreas Fault, that junction of two giant plates of the earth whose movements occasionally preoccupy residents of the Southland.

Turn up Big Pines Highway, County Road N4, and follow it along the fault line and through an often overlooked, but very pretty, section of the National Forest. You'll pass campgrounds, picnic areas, and Jackson Lake, a natural sag pond (it doesn't drain) and popular puddle for swimming or shore-fishing.

The road descends quickly from Jackson Lake and at many of its S-turns opens onto views of the high desert. Joshua trees begin to fraternize with the pines here, a good indication that you're losing altitude. You'll soon come to

Prodigious yucca—this one nearly 20 feet high—flourish in the dry, chaparral-covered canyons of the San Gabriels.

Mile High Cafe, a little country diner where you can sidle up to the counter for a burger, play some pinball, or have a cool drink on a covered patio. At Valyermo (the word means "desert valley"), the road bottoms out and you're on the desert floor. Sort of. Thanks to the presence of Big Rock Creek and natural springs, the valley is lush and irrigated and doesn't look much like desert. Cottonwood trees follow the stream courses, fields are planted in alfalfa, and orchards produce peaches, pears, apples, and cherries. A ranger station and a post office comprise "downtown" Valyermo.

To get to Devil's Punchbowl, turn left on Pallett Creek Road and follow the signs that lead you up Longview and Devil's Punchbowl Road to the entrance to Devil's Punchbowl County Park.

If you haven't seen too much in the way of earthquake faulting to this point, you're forgiven. Through much of the rift zone, the evidence is subtle. But at Devil's Punchbowl, which is actually on a nearby subsidiary fault, the earth's forces are in your face. Faulting and erosion have created contorted shapes out of ancient sedimentary rocks and alluvial deposits. A viewpoint behind the visitor's center looks down into the satanic amphitheater, and a mile-long loop trail takes you down to "hell" and back.

From Devil's Punchbowl, retrace your way back down Longview Road. Take time to admire the thick stands of Joshua trees—in few places are the trees quite so sociable. Turn left on Fort Tejon Road and follow it toward Littlerock. Our route back to the Angeles will turn left on Mount

Contorted rock formations of Devil's Punchbowl evidence the forces at work along the nearby San Andreas Fault.

Emma Road, but it's only a mile into the town of Littlerock, a worthwhile detour. Along the way you'll cross the California Aqueduct and get a good look at this amazing artificial artery that carries water from the Sacramento/San Joaquin Delta to slake Los Angeles's thirst. Believe it or not, fishing is permitted here. Tossing a line into a cement river seems to me to be a slightly odd, even sad, pastime, but maybe the fishing's good. In any event, the produce in Littlerock and in neighboring Pearblossom is definitely good. Farmers' markets in the towns sell the wonderful fruits that grow in abundance around here.

Back across the aqueduct, turn west on Mount Emma Road, also called the Littlerock Cutoff. A side road leads to Little Rock Reservoir. Otherwise, this is a quiet, little-traveled and uninterrupted road that climbs gently out of scrub sage (and lush grasses in spring) into the pinyon belt and back into the Angeles National Forest. Turn left on Angeles Forest Highway, which peaks out at Mill Creek Summit (4,910 feet) then levels out along Mill Creek and enters Hidden Springs. Here we pick up the route described below.

UPPER BIG TUJUNGA CANYON

Upper Big Tujunga Canyon Road slides gently down from the Angeles Crest into the broad canyon of the same name. As is the case in most San Gabriel Mountains canyons, the hot south-facing slopes are dry chaparral; the cool north-facing slopes are shady pine forest. Soon it's all arid chaparral and chalky limestone soil—almost as if the scenery had been decolorized to black-and-white.

After several miles of descending, Upper Big Tujunga joins Angeles Forest Highway (County Road N3). Turn left. If you're sensing that the wide upper canyon and various side canyons are converging, you're right. And so are the tributary streams that flow through them and into the Tujunga River. Angeles Forest Highway parallels one of

Impressive road engineering makes backroad travel possible through the rugged San Gabriels—here, Big Tujunga Canyon Road.

these converging tributaries, the Middle Fork of Mill Creek. You can't really see the little burble of a creek—it flows through a gorge about 20 feet deep as it passes through the tiny settlement of Hidden Springs. But that placid gorge was once the site of terror and destruction.

When you stop for a cider or a piece of pie at Hidden Springs Cafe, ask Elva Lewis what happened here in 1978. As you relax in the tranquil setting, she'll tell you about the dry-season chaparral fire and the winter storm a few months later that sent not just a flood but a tidal wave of debris funneling into this canyon, tearing out homes, and washing away cars, trucks, and people. Her husband Amos saved his life by grabbing a tree limb after the debris flow lifted him nearly out of the gorge. John McPhee graphically describes the flood in his book *Control of Nature*.

Fire and flood create a timeless cycle in the San Gabriels, which are largely composed of crumbly rock particularly vulnerable to sliding, to earthquakes, and to the force of moving water. The 1978 flood was typical, for when winter storms pelt the mountains, especially after a fire, the runoff carries away tons of mountain—even huge boulders.

The bridge across The Narrows of the Big Tujunga River stands 200 feet above the wild canyon bottom, but passing motorists must debark to appreciate its scale.

Although the flows created the ground on which the foothill communities are built, the local flood control district labors constantly to keep those very towns from being inundated.

Continue down the Angeles Forest Highway to the place known as The Narrows of the Big Tujunga, a dramatic, deep gorge carved from solid rock. After you pass through a tunnel and cross a bridge, you can park and walk back across the bridge to a viewing platform. Only then do you realize how high (200 feet) above The Narrows the bridge passes. You can hear the wind swishing the cottonwoods far below, but the trees look like miniatures.

Stay with the canyon by turning right where the sign says, simply, "Big T Canyon." The road follows a shelf blasted out of steep rock cliffs, and descends steeply. Pull over at an early turnout and you'll see a reservoir deep in the canyon, backed up by Big Tujunga Dam, one of many in the

San Gabriels built to hold back debris flows from the foothill communities. But even the huge Big T Dam can be overwhelmed, as it was in 1938 when a torrent overflowed the spillway and washed away hundreds of cabins below—the same storm that wiped out Switzer-Land in the Arroyo Seco.

Most likely you'll see nothing more than a pleasant flow of the Big Tujunga River below the dam, trickling through a rocky bed many times wider than the river. Where it levels out near the town of Tujunga, some fine swimming holes form, and on a warm day you'll see a lot of city dwellers cooling off and giving little thought to the latent force the stream represents.

Big T Road becomes Oro Vista in the town of Tujunga and joins Foothill Boulevard about eight miles from where this tour started. Turn right to meet Interstate 210 and go east on 210 to return to the Glendale Freeway.

The Castaic Mountains: The "Other" Angeles National Forest

86 miles
Palmdale • Leona Valley • Bouquet Canyon • San Francisquito Canyon • Lake Elizabeth • Lake Hughes • Elizabeth Lake Canyon • Lake Castaic

The mountainous triangle bordered on the west by Interstate 5, the east by State Highway 14, and the north by County Road N2 (which parallels the San Andreas Fault) is often overlooked as part of the Angeles National Forest. Whether this northwest corner of the forest is also the northwest corner of the San Gabriel Mountains is a matter of some dispute. Most maps place the San Gabriels to the east of Highway 14, and in this area identify only the individual ridges. The unofficial designation "Castaic Mountains" groups together the various ridges and canyons that comprise this tour.

Although two modern boom towns—Santa Clarita and Palmdale—crowd the fringes of this area, the towns within the triangle retain a quiet village atmosphere, and backroads that follow rugged canyons provide access to camp-grounds and cool, shady streams. Add to that the site of Southern California's worst man-caused disaster plus one of Southern California's most popular recreational lakes, and you've got a pretty full tour.

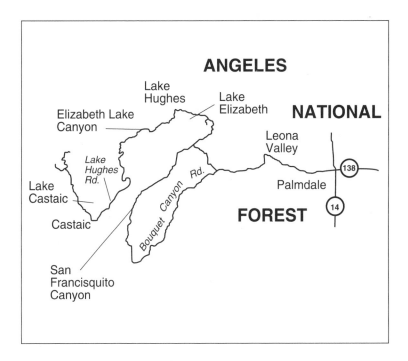

To begin the tour: From Los Angeles, take Interstate 5 (Golden State Freeway) north to State Highway 14 (Antelope Valley Freeway) toward Palmdale. Before you proceed into Palmdale, take a moment to pause at the Lamont Odett Vista Point just south of town, where you get a view of Palmdale Lake and the California Aqueduct, which sweeps from west to east along the San Andreas

Fault. Exit at Palmdale Boulevard (State Highway 138) and turn left on what becomes Elizabeth Lake Road.

Once you clear some Palmdale tracts, you enter the very pretty Leona Valley, a surprisingly lush, grassy basin drained by the Amaragosa River. The river is marked by a line of cottonwood trees, and many of the big oaks on the basin floor are deciduous valley oaks, so the fall brings a brilliant yellow contrast to the surrounding evergreen chaparral. If you don't get a strong sense, as you drive along, of being on the cusp of two massive earth plates, don't despair. It takes a geologist's eye to distinctly see the evidence, but believe it: You're precisely on the San Andreas Fault. The Pacific Ocean side of the fault is moving northward relative to the Antelope Valley and the interior. All that subterranean force building up has no effect on the serenity of the setting, where irrigated fields of alfalfa wave in the breeze, orchards flourish, and horses graze in natural pasture.

After five miles, turn left on Bouquet Canyon Road which runs between rounded, chaparral-covered hills and more shady fruit orchards. You'll soon come upon Bouquet Reservoir. It looks quite inviting, but a chain-link and barbed-wire fence surrounding it plainly rescinds the imaginary invitation. Bouquet is what's called a seasonal regulating reservoir, holding Owens Valley drinking water for a thirsty Los Angeles basin.

Below Bouquet Canyon Dam, the road closely follows Bouquet Creek into a canyon so narrow in places that there's just room for the creek and the road. Along the wider stretches, country homes and cabins line the creek, many of them utilizing distinctive Bouquet Canyon flagstone. Some of the prettiest homes in the canyon are just upstream from The Falls, a 25-foot waterfall. The stone homes seem to be almost part of the stream and the cas-

This northern stretch of Bouquet Canyon Road leads through rugged chaparral-covered mountains into shady Bouquet Canyon.

cade. A succession of small forest service campgrounds follows, and Big Oaks Cafe makes a shady rest stop for locals, travelers, and weekend-warrior bikers. So close to Palmdale and Santa Clarita, this bucolic heart of Bouquet Canyon seems decades removed in time.

Lower Bouquet Canyon opens into farmland, a reminder of an old way of life here before Santa Clarita swallowed the town of Saugus and began a determined march up the country canyons north of town. You'll now have to make a swing through the 'burbs to get to the next canyon road. Continue south on Bouquet Canyon to Seco Canyon Road. Turn right, then right on San Francisquito Canyon Road.

DISASTER SITE

As you begin up the broad lower portion of San Francisquito Canyon, nothing hints at the awful tragedy that struck here on March 12, 1928. You have to go farther up-canyon, and even there, you have to be determined and curious to find evidence of the flood that washed all the way to the Pacific in Ventura and carried away at least 450 bodies (most were never found), 1,200 homes and numerous orchards, farms and ranches.

The flood ensued when the poorly constructed Saint Francis Dam gave way and a 200-foot wall of water rushed through the narrow canyon (imagine this as you drive up-canyon), through the towns of Castaic Junction, Piru, and Fillmore, and along the course of the Santa Clara River to the ocean. The dam was the brainchild of William Mulholland, megalomaniacal kingpin of the system of aqueducts and reservoirs that purloin water from Northern California to water the lawns and golf courses of Southern California. Dams like Saint Francis were built to contain water that poured south from the Owens River, but Saint Francis was hastily built and poorly designed—and Chief Engineer Mulholland chose to ignore warning signs on the eve of the disaster. "I envy the dead," he said afterward.

I commend you to Mark Reisner's book *Cadillac Desert* for the full, odious story of Los Angeles water politics and

This pile of rubble is all that's left of the Saint Francis Dam, which gave way in 1928. The ensuing wall of water killed at least 450 and swept away 1,200 homes. The view looks north toward the would-be reservoir, with San Francisquito Canyon Road visible in the background.

a vivid description of the Saint Francis Dam disaster. But it's important to know that Los Angeles is really a desert city, drier than Beirut, and that its greenery and its teeming population are watered at terrific expense. In the case of the Saint Francis dam, a human toll was added to that expense. The movie *Chinatown* also takes its story line from the greed and shenanigans behind Los Angeles water politics.

No signs, memorials, or anything else point the way or commemorate what happened here in 1928, but the Saint Francis Dam site is reasonably easy to find. Continue 1.5 miles north of the San Francisquito ranger station, cross over a bridge, and park immediately in a turnout on the left. The path to the dam site, which takes about 10 minutes to walk, leads uphill from underneath a large oak tree. The view both up and down the canyon is poignantly placid. All you'll see of the dam is a high ridge strewn with chunks of concrete and twisted strands of steel rebar. But it's an appropriate tribute to the Faustian ingenuity and audacity that brought water to Los Angeles in 1913, and disaster in 1928.

Of course, it still takes large measures of ingenuity and audacity to bring water to Southern California. Just up from the dam site you'll see San Francisquito Power Plant No. 1, into which run giant pipelines. The pipelines are part of the L.A. Aqueduct system which carries High Sierra water from distant Owens Valley. It's a deft stroke of planning that the water is used to spin turbines in two power plants before it runs south into the L.A. Reservoir in San Fernando and then to the metropolitan drinking water system.

San Francisquito Canyon Road becomes increasingly more dramatic as it ascends the steep-walled, V-shaped canyon. Near the crest, a side trip into Green Valley is worthwhile. This hidden little town consists of shaded homes, a store or two, a lot of horses, and orchards, insulated in a dell between high mountain ridges. The name comes from the abundant live oaks that shade and cool the town. On the other side of town is Spunky Canyon, where there's a quiet, isolated campground. The road eventually joins Bouquet Canyon at the reservoir.

San Francisquito Canyon continues north to intersect Lake Elizabeth Road, where you'll turn left toward Lake Elizabeth.

ELIZABETH AND HUGHES

At first, Lake Elizabeth appears to be nothing but a private country club, but the west end of the lake is in the national forest and has good trout fishing and a day use area. It's a natural lake, so its level fluctuates by season and by year.

Just beyond Elizabeth you come into the town of Lake Hughes and the body of water of the same name. The lake is in private hands, but an American Adventures RV resort called Forest Lakes provides nice camping and picnicking facilities and overnight trailer rentals.

The most distinctive building in the town of Lake Hughes is the Rock Inn, a stone edifice right on the main road that contains a hotel and a roadhouse-type tavern/restaurant—the type of place where you dine amid the din of country music and a lot of happy locals.

HUGHES TO CASTAIC

Now for a confusion of nomenclature. You've been on Lake Elizabeth Road which runs by Lake Hughes. Now, turn left on Lake Hughes Road which runs to Lake Castaic through, get this, Lake Elizabeth Canyon. Go figure.

Anyway, it's another dramatic canyon drive as it descends the canyon generally southward, passing by private camps and forest service campgrounds. At first, the walls of the canyon crowd the road and hover above the resident stream along which stand sycamores, alders, cottonwoods, and willows. At Cottonwood Campground the canyon broadens, and from here down are sweeping views to the south and west of receding ridges of the rugged transverse ranges that extend westward to the ocean.

At your first glimpse of Castaic Lake, pull into a turnout and you can see the road ahead following a long, arcing ridge down to the lake. All along this ridge are more views of the lake that fills long fingers of rugged arroyos far below.

Finally, at the bottom, is access to Castaic Lake State Recreation Area. Castaic is a product of the California State Water Project—a different system from the one you saw in San Francisquito Canyon. Castaic water comes from the Sacramento/San Joaquin Delta and is pumped, incredibly, over the Tehachapi Mountains north of here into Quail Lake. The aqueduct then splits—the east branch flows into Pyramid and Castaic, and the west branch through the Antelope Valley to Silverwood Lake, as you saw from the Highway 14 Lamont Odett Vista Point at the start of this tour.

This view from Lake Hughes Road looks northwest across Castaic Mountains toward distant Mount Pinos. Castaic Lake is hidden from view in the near canyon.

Only an hour or so from about a trillion people, Castaic is a very popular lake for boating, bass fishing, and wind-surfing, but, like other reservoirs of drinking water, allows no swimming. It also has a couple of RV campgrounds.

At road's end, you have two choices: You can take Interstate 5 back to Los Angeles, or you can turn right on the Old Road which parallels I-5 for seven miles, a lower section of the Old Ridge Route that once snaked tortuously up and over the Grapevine. At Templin Highway, you can continue a bit farther to a viewpoint above Castaic Lake or turn left to I-5 for the return to Los Angeles.

TOUR 7

The San Bernardino Mountains

110 miles
*Cajon Pass • Lake Silverwood • Rim of the World Drive •
Lake Arrowhead • Big Bear Lake • Holcomb Valley •
Onyx Summit • Angelus Oaks • Redlands*

Backroads driving has long been a way of life in the San
Bernardino Mountains. Although it was lumbering and
gold that lured the first white settlers into the mountains in
the 1860s, tourism followed shortly behind. A toll road
completed in 1892 made the mountain crest accessible from
San Bernardino, a stage line began operating in 1896, and
resorts like the Squirrel Inn and Arrowhead Springs Hotel
brought a steady flow of visitors seeking to escape summer
heat or to frolic in the snow.

The flow has never slowed. The San Bernardinos are much
more developed than the San Gabriels or the San Jacintos.
The resort communities like Arrowhead and Big Bear Lake
can seem at times like pine-shaded facsimiles of Los Angeles
suburbs. But the mountains also contain great wild spaces
and one of the world's truly great mountain roads.

It was the completion in 1915 of that road, Rim of the World Drive, that ushered in the era of motor touring in the San Bernardinos. The spectacular, 101-mile route up from San Bernardino and across the crest of the mountains remains one of the most compelling mountain roads anywhere, with its sinuous precipice overlooking the San Bernardino Valley and the world. The Forest Service has designated a Scenic Byway that incorporates most of the Rim of the World and links many of the resorts and accessible natural areas of the San Bernardino Mountains. This tour traces, for the most part, the Forest Service's Rim of the World Scenic Byway.

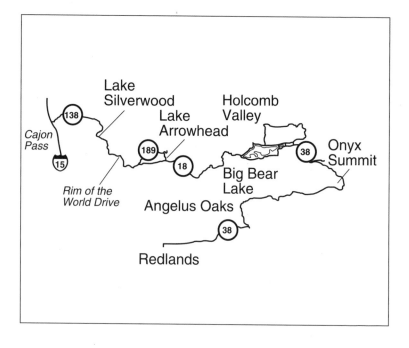

To begin the tour: Take Interstate 10 east from Los Angeles to Interstate 15 north. Midway through the Cajon Pass, exit on State Highway 138 and turn right (east).

CAJON PASS

Cajon Pass, a natural break between the San Gabriel and San Bernardino Mountains, is one of Southern California's most historic travel corridors. It carried Spaniards to the San Bernardino Valley where they established huge cattle ranches, the Mormons to San Bernardino where they established the town, and Indian raiders who made easy pickings of the Spanish cattle and horses.

As Highway 138 winds through bunchgrass and chaparral, it parallels the Santa Fe Railroad tracks for a while, then crests, leaving behind the pass to enter Horsethief Canyon. A Ute Indian called Walkara once enlisted the help of mountain man Peg Leg Smith (our old friend who discovered gold in Anza-Borrego; see Tour 16) in purloining some 5,000 horses from the Spanish and driving them through this canyon—hence the name. This is still ranch country. The Las Flores Ranch in Summit Valley off to the left (north) has been running cattle here since 1862. As the road rises again, bright yellow Spanish broom lines the pavement and scents the air. Soon the road enters San Bernardino National Forest and opens onto a view of Silverwood Lake.

SILVERWOOOD LAKE

Silverwood is part of the giant plumbing works known as the California State Water Project. It's very simple, really. Snow falls in the northern Sierra Nevada, melts, flows into the Feather River Basin (680 miles north), pauses at Oroville Dam, then heads down the Feather and Sacramento Rivers into the California Aqueduct, flows down the San Joaquin Valley, then gets pumped 1,926 feet up over the Tehachapis, then splits off. One branch slakes Los Angeles; the other gets pumped up again from Pearblossom to 3,480 feet above sea level, then gets piped under the Mojave River and into Silverwood Lake. The poor water doesn't get much of a rest, though. From Silverwood, its exciting journey passes through a 3.8-mile tunnel, plunges 1,600 feet, generates some electricity, then finally drops, exhausted, into Lake Perris, south of Riverside. Whew. That's what we go through in Southern California to get a drink of water.

Anyway, Silverwood is a fine place for camping and fishing. In contrast to the heavy development around Arrowhead and Big Bear lakes, Silverwood is surrounded by state-operated parkland. Campgrounds are shaded by big oaks, and tall pines form a stately fringe on the rim of the basin overlooking the lake. Fishing is good here for catfish, rainbow trout, crappie, and striped and largemouth bass, although anglers must share the lake with speedboats and waterskiers.

ON TO ARROWHEAD

Highway 138 climbs as it leaves Silverwood, finally entering cool forests of pines and oaks and leaving behind the thick, brushy chaparral of the lower slopes. The road snakes through these forests, passes through small cabin communities, then meets State Highway 18 on the southern flank of the mountain range. Turn left, and you're on Rim of the World Drive. There's no questioning the appropriateness of the name, but it's best to savor the experience from a turnout or from nearby Baylis Park, a Forest Service picnic area. Depending on conditions, you might see forever, or you might see a gauze of smog lying over San Bernardino and the urban basin. Quite often the basin is covered with coastal fog and clouds in the morning. You'll break through the clouds at some point on Rim of the World and see San Bernardino Peak looming ahead of you to the east and Santiago Peak in the Santa Ana Mountains to the southwest, looking like a floating island.

Shortly after Baylis Park, turn left on Daley Canyon Road which joins State Highway 189, passes through the little

Whether the basin below is clear or fogged in, pull-outs along Rim of the World Drive offer true precipice-of-the-planet views.

town of Blue Jay (home of an Olympic-size ice skating rink), and leads to Lake Arrowhead. The original purpose of the lake when the basin was dammed in 1906 was to irrigate the San Bernardino Valley. Desert ranchers along the Mojave River, into which the natural drainage flowed, brought suit to halt the hijacking of their water. They won. The lake became a resort in the 1920s, a faux-Swiss village that drew Hollywood rich and famous and sat in for European villages in a number of old movies. The original village was replaced by a new one in 1981. Although the village retained the timbered architecture of the original, it feels synthetic and citified to me. The 38-acre complex includes a 261-room resort and a McDonald's, as well as a lot of shops and a few restaurants overlooking the lake. Still standing in the midst of it all is the spire-topped old Pavilion where visitors once danced to Glenn Miller and Tommy Dorsey, but today it's given over to a variety of boutiques.

Rich, green mixed conifer forest surrounds Lake Arrowhead, and flowering dogwoods are abundant and evident in spring. But most of the lake shoreline is in private hands, with no public access or boating. If you want to get out on the lake, you can take a 50-minute scenic cruise aboard the *Arrowhead Queen*, which leaves from the village marina.

THE ROAD TO BIG BEAR

From Lake Arrowhead, return to Rim of the World Drive by way of Highway 173. Now it's 27 miles of driving through pine forests and along the precipice of the planet from Arrowhead to Big Bear. Shortly after you rejoin the drive, you'll come to the Arrowhead District ranger station where you can pick up information on camping and hiking in the area. Although the stunning view often lures your gaze away, the forests of the mountain crest really are magnificent: sugar and coulter pines with their huge cones, ponderosa and Jeffrey pines, and white fir and incense cedars, with deciduous black oaks and dogwoods stirred into the mixture. Be sure to take a walk *somewhere* in the San Bernardinos. As in the San Gabriels, a John Robinson guidebook is a must for hikers. His *San Bernardino Mountain Trails* describes 100 hikes in the national forest. In the Arrowhead area, Deep Creek, a perennial stream with deep pools, offers some great hiking and flyfishing. Access is from Cedar Glen, east of Lake Arrowhead Village.

For an easy, short walk beside the road, pull over at Heaps Peak Arboretum. The forest represents a rebirth after a 1922 fire. With trail pamphlet in hand, you can get acquainted with the trees of the San Bernardino National Forest, including a showy dogwood grove near trail's end.

From here, the highway passes through the town of Running Springs which has places to eat and stay, then enters Snow Valley where there's a ski area and a winter playground. Shortly after Snow Valley, the road climbs along a major divide and tops out at Lake View Point, 7,117 feet, where you get your first view of Big Bear Lake, still six miles to the northeast. The last few miles are curving and twisting ones. Finally, the road dodges some huge boulders and deposits you on the shore of Big Bear Lake.

BIG BEAR LAKE

Although black bears still lurk in the San Bernardino Mountains forests, Big Bear takes its name from the extinct California grizzly. Benjamin Davis Wilson, for whom Mount Wilson was named, headed an 1845 hunting party that brought in 22 grizzlies in two days. He decided to call the high mountain basin Bear Valley. The lake came later, when the first dam was built in 1884. It was supplanted by a larger one in 1910.

Big Bear is somewhat more user-friendly than Arrowhead. Its towns may be a little worn at the edges, but visitors feel comfortable and welcome; there's plenty of lake access at 10 marinas and two public boat launches, plus there's dining and lodging of all sorts at all prices. The lake is seven miles long, about a half-mile wide, and is stocked with trout, bass, coho salmon, and catfish. The lake is also popular for waterskiing, jet-skiing, sailing, and windsurfing, and swimming is allowed within 50 feet of shore.

The highway meets the lake at its southwest corner where you have a choice of going left on State Highway 38 around the northern, less developed shore or staying right and continuing on Big Bear Boulevard through the town of Big Bear Lake. I recommend a circle tour.

QUIET NORTH SHORE

Highway 38 hugs the north shoreline and offers some fine views of Big Bear's alpine setting, with 9,000-foot peaks forming a backdrop behind the town. You'll pass a marina and boat launch and the quiet community of Fawnskin. If it happens to be dinnertime, Pepino's restaurant in Fawnskin is a "find" for good homemade Italian food served by the gregarious, aria-belting owner.

Beyond Fawnskin, you might glimpse an apparition that looks like a white dome out in the water. This is the Big Bear Solar Observatory of the California Institute of Technology. Turn right on North Shore Lane to get a closer look. The site was chosen for Big Bear's high percentage of sunlight (330 sunny days a year), and particularly stable atmosphere above the surface of the lake. Personally, I wonder about the condition of the corneas of astronomers staring at the sun all day. Tours are offered on Saturdays during the summer. Just don't stare too long.

North Shore Lane also leads to Big Bear North Campground and some lakefront picnic areas. These, and a gentle, three-mile bike path, are all part of the North Shore Recreation Area. The lane soon rejoins Highway 38, and you'll quickly come to the Big Bear District Ranger Station, the info-dispensing headquarters for this neck of the national forest. In winter, inquire here about bald eagle tours. Our national bird graces all the lakes in this area during the winter months.

HOLCOMB VALLEY GOLD FEVER TOUR

If you're feeling adventurous, pick up the Forest Service's Gold Fever Trail self-guided auto tour brochure and take a side trip into Holcomb Valley. The 12-mile trip is entirely by dirt road, rough at times, but passable by two-wheel drive in summer. Holcomb Valley was a hotbed of mining activity in the 1860s and 1870s, and this tour takes in some reminders of the era: ruins of cabins and a saloon, panning streams, mine shafts, and the obligatory hangman's tree. The tour begins a mile west of the ranger station, up Poligue Canyon Road.

A tiny miner's cabin in Holcomb Valley is a reminder of the Big Bear area's brief gold rush of 1860-61.

It may surprise you to learn that gold fever lingers even today. Holcomb Valley is studded with claims (marked by posts or piles of rocks), and anyone can gold-pan in the streams (outside of claims). However, the Forest Service warns against entering mine tunnels "as they may contain shafts and/or bad air. YOU COULD BE DEAD BEFORE YOU REALIZE IT." And who wants that?

The gold tour is interesting, but Holcomb Valley's appeal to me is its serenity—perhaps a semblance of what Bear Valley was 150 years ago—and the rugs of rare dwarf wildflowers that splash color among the tall pine trees in spring and early summer.

Whether by way of Holcomb Valley or by continuing on Highway 38, you'll eventually pass the east end of Big Bear Lake and come down upon Baldwin Lake. Baldwin is dry or barely wet much of the time, and there's no recreation allowed on it, but the natural lake is important as a site for wintering birds, as an ecological preserve for rare wildflowers, and for a rare fish called the unarmored three-spined stickleback. At the northeast end of Baldwin Lake, Highway

18 leaves Big Bear Valley and drops down to Lucerne Valley in the high desert (see Tour 15). Turn back here, and follow Highway 18 into the town of Big Bear Lake.

THE DEVELOPED SIDE

Big Bear Lake is more woodsy than fancy, but it has all the amenities of a mountain resort, including two ski areas: Bear Mountain and Snow Summit, which bring big crowds of skiers to Big Bear on winter weekends. Coming from Baldwin Lake on Highway 18, turn left (south) on Moonridge Drive to reach Bear Mountain. Turn left on Summit Boulevard to reach Snow Summit.

By summer, Snow Summit has become one of the country's hotbeds for mountain biking. Mountain bikers can buy an all-day pass to ride the lifts and to pedal forest roads and trails in the mountains. Bikes are available at Team Big Bear at the base of the lifts, or at Big Bear Bikes down the hill on Highway 18 (Big Bear Boulevard). The shops can suggest many other places to ride. Holcomb Valley is particularly pleasant for easy riding. Of course, you don't have to have

Several marinas provide access to and, just as importantly, the inside scoop about, Big Bear Lake's excellent fishing.

a mountain bike with you to ride the Scenic Sky Chair at Snow Summit during the summer. At the top, you can walk in the high woods and enjoy an aerial view of the lake.

Back on level ground, continue west on Big Bear Boulevard, which is lined with businesses for miles. Pine Knot Avenue, with its mountain village feeling, is the other major commercial street.

One block east of Pine Knot Avenue, on Knickerbocker Road, is Big Bear's most historic hostelry, the Knickerbocker Mansion. The mansion is a four-story log house, at once rustic and elegant, surrounded by lawn and pines and commanding a view of the lake. It and the carriage house out back comprise a romantic bed-and-breakfast inn.

The circle tour of the lake passes by Boulder Bay, a pretty, boulder-strewn cove, then returns you to the junction of Highways 18 and 38 at Big Bear Dam. Traffic may be the deciding factor on which way to backtrack, but to continue the tour, go east on 18 or 38, pass the lake, and remain on Highway 38 through the town of Big Bear City.

Big carved bears are ubiquitous icons around Big Bear Lake. This one lords over Sugarloaf Cordwood, whose owner, Robert Wyrick, carves the creatures with a chain saw.

As you may have noticed on your drive around the lake, it's virtually obligatory for residents and businesses alike to own a carved wooden bear. The den where most of these bears come from is a business called Sugarloaf Cordwood. Owner Robert Wyrick is a chainsaw bear-carver, and his work, as well as that of other carvers, is on sale here at the corner of Big Bear Boulevard and Stanfield Cutoff.

TO ONYX SUMMIT AND DOWN

Highway 38 heads south out of Big Bear City and begins making a long circumnavigation of Sugarloaf Mountain (9,952 feet), the massive peak that dominates the view along this stretch of the tour. Here in the lee of Sugarloaf, the landscape is sparse and dry, with scattered pinyon and juniper—more characteristic of the high desert than 8,000-foot mountains. The road crests at Onyx Summit and descends, following dramatic road cuts and dropping into a lusher, wetter sector of the range. Turnouts offer views of the canyon of the Santa Ana River. Across the way, you can see the long, steep switchback of the Clark Grade, the old route from the Santa Ana River valley to Big Bear. The hot, steep climb boiled over a lot of Model T radiators in the '20s, and the road was so narrow it operated under a control system: uphill traffic for three hours, then downhill traffic for the next three. Our "back door to Big Bear" Highway 38 was not completed beyond Barton Flats until 1961.

The road soon meets and parallels Cienega Seca Creek and then the Santa Ana River, where aspens grow and turn golden in the fall. Heart Bar and the complex of forest service campgrounds in Barton Flats near the Santa Ana River offer some of the best camping in the San Bernardinos, with shady sites beneath tall pines. Scout and youth camps are also scattered throughout the Barton Flats area.

SHADOW OF SAN GORGONIO

As you travel here between Heart Bar and Barton Flats, you're due north of the summit of that great hulk of a mountain, San Gorgonio (also known as Old Grayback, at 11,499 feet the highest in Southern California). The forest surrounding the mountain is all wilderness area, so you'll need a permit to enter it or to climb the peak. A number of trails lead up the mountain, all of them difficult, but the true alpine environment, virgin forests, and the top-of-the-world view make San Gorgonio a mecca for hearty Southern California peak-baggers.

Beyond Barton Flats, the scenic byway descends through the old resort community of Angelus Oaks. ("Angelus" is not a misspelling, but rather a Roman Catholic prayer.) As it continues descending, pine trees give way quickly to oaks and chaparral, except for some big-cone spruce in the side canyons. After a few sweeping curves, the road bottoms and meets boulder-strewn Mill Creek. A short detour to the left leads to Forest Falls Picnic Area and Big Falls, one of the best waterfalls in Southern California. Continue down Highway 38 and pause at the vista point to contemplate your surroundings. Two facts of interest about Mill Creek and its canyon: The creek was the site of a pioneer hydroelectric plant built in 1893 to light up nearby Redlands. Southern California Edison still operates three powerhouses on Mill Creek. Also consider that you're standing directly on the North Branch of the San Andreas Fault. The slot-like canyon you see to the east was not carved by Mill Creek, but was a matter of the stream finding its way through a line of fault-weakened rock.

The denouement of this tour is anticlimactic. The road follows Mill Creek awhile, then descends a rocky fan to Redlands, where you have no choice but to endure several miles of suburbia before you reach Interstate 10 for the return drive.

TOUR 8

Idyllwild, Palm Springs, and the San Jacintos

100 miles
*Banning • Idyllwild • Palms to Pines Highway • Palm
Desert • Palm Springs • Palm Springs Aerial Tramway •
San Gorgonio Pass • Windmills*

Mount San Jacinto, second tallest mountain in Southern
California, is familiar to many as the backdrop to Palm
Springs and its contiguous desert resorts. And for travelers
approaching Southern California from the east, San Jacinto
is half of an empyrean portal to the promised land, along
with Mount San Gorgonio on the other side of San Gorgonio
Pass. This tour loops around Mount San Jacinto, climbs into
its range, then drops down to the Coachella Valley and finally returns to the very lap of the grand mountain. The route
epitomizes the grand-scale juxtapositions of Southern
California: tall mountain and low desert, and enduring natural beauty in the face of mass development.

To begin the tour: Take Interstate 10 east from Los Angeles
about 85 miles to Banning. Take the Idyllwild/State
Highway 243 exit and follow the signs toward Idyllwild.

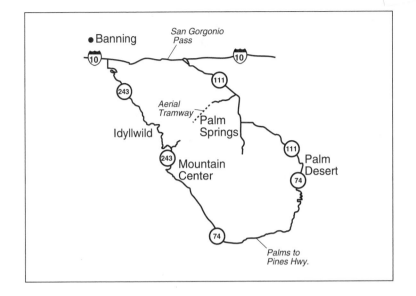

SCENIC HIGHWAY

State Highway 243 is an officially designated state scenic highway, as if this scenery needs the endorsement. The road begins climbing immediately from its start in windswept San Gorgonio Pass, and you're soon in quite a different world from the freeway corridor. We have Colonel M.S. Hall to thank for this and many other San Jacinto routes. The colonel was a grading contractor for the Southern Pacific who brought the railroad through this pass in 1876. His search for timber—for railroad ties, that is—took him up into the mountains where he etched roads and built a few sawmills. His wagon roads were improved over the years, but this route was still a steep, rough track until paving and grading was completed in 1948. With prisoners and WPA workers providing labor, it took 13 years to build. It was opened to much fanfare and clumsily dubbed "The Banning to Idyllwild Panoramic Highway." Now it's just Highway 243, or Idyllwild Road.

It's a wonderful road, snaking around the contours of the northern shoulders of the mountains and offering a new view around every bend. It plays tricks of perspective on you—at first you see San Gorgonio across the pass on your left, then it's on your right. It begins in chaparral country. In spring, in addition to dense scrub oak, you'll see luxuriant grasses and fluffy blossoms of ceanothus, that nondescript staple of chaparral that in spring earns its alternate name, California lilac. Turnouts enable you to safely appreciate the views to the west; if the basin is cloudy or hazy, you're in luck. You'll see a set of ridges piercing the cloud layer and disappearing toward the Pacific. If the basin is clear, you see the urban sprawl. If the basin is smoggy, keep driving.

You're in the pine zone now, in the San Bernardino National Forest, and you'll soon come to a turnout at Bay Tree Spring where you can fill your water bottles with delicious spring water. This kind of ritual is an old-fashioned backroads tradition that has been largely displaced by synthesized rest stops on the interstates. But imagine how welcome the spring was to early travelers on the hot, dusty road to Idyllwild.

Just as welcoming is little Lake Fulmor, tucked off to the left of an S-bend in the road and a shady spot for a picnic or swim. Beyond the lake is a turnoff for Black Mountain, a dirt road that twists four miles uphill to a National Forest campground, one of many off Highway 243 in the San Jacintos.

IDYLLWILD

Idyllwild is almost as pleasant as its name. Beautifully situated at 5,400 feet beneath Tahquitz Mountain (8,828 feet) and Suicide Rock, it has all the trappings of a mountain resort —tall pines, plenty of places to eat and stay, and shops with cute names selling cute things. Most of the development is pretty tasteful, in keeping with the woodsy nature of the place. Probably because it has no lake or ski area, Idyllwild has retained its character as a place of retreat, although if you spend all your time in downtown, you'll want to retreat from the retreat.

Fortunately, you have many alternatives. Idyllwild is a jumping-off spot for some terrific hiking trails. Just west of the city limits on your way into town is Idyllwild County Park, which has a small visitor center with good nature and history exhibits. Across the highway from the park is the trailhead for Deer Springs Trail that leads three and a half miles uphill to Suicide Rock. You might think the name relates somehow to the rock climbers who scale its face, but its origin has to do with a legend of Indian lovers who jumped to their deaths. The towering monoliths of Suicide Rock and Tahquitz are summer hangouts for rock climbers who spend winter and spring in Joshua Tree National Monument.

Ranger stations for both the San Bernardino National Forest and Mount San Jacinto State Park are on opposite sides of the highway in Idyllwild. I heartily recommend a hike out of Humber Park, a county park above town; but if you plan to venture into the state wilderness, you must pick up a permit from the state park office. Devil's Slide Trail out of Humber Park is a challenging ascent into the high country. The Ernie Maxwell Trail is a gentler walk in the woods that requires no permit, or you can just dangle your toes in Strawberry Creek as it babbles through Humber Park. If you're a peak-bagger, the trailhead for the South Ridge Trail to Tahquitz is just out of town on South Ridge Road. You need a permit anyway, so get a map and directions from the state park office. Hint: If you want to get into the highest of San Jacinto high country, wait until the end of this tour and begin your hike from atop the Palms Springs Aerial Tramway.

One landmark in town worth noting (and hard to miss) is the Idyllwild Tree Monument—a totem pole that rises from

The landmark 50-foot totem pole in the heart of Idyllwild was carved by a chainsaw from a single pine tree.

the center of town. Artist Jonathan LaBenne used a chainsaw (seven of them, actually) to carve it from a single pine tree. Crowning the 50-foot pole is a 10-foot bald eagle, and peering out of the back through a knothole is Ernie Maxwell, Idyllwild's town crier, publisher of the local paper (*The Town Crier*), and a local landmark in his own right.

As you continue on Highway 243 through Idyllwild you will see on the edge of town the entrance to the Idyllwild School of Music and the Arts (ISOMATA), a 200-acre campus affiliated with the University of Southern California. Performances and classes in the arts at ISOMATA are a summer tradition in Idyllwild.

PALMS TO PINES

From Idyllwild, Highway 243 descends to the little crossroads town of Mountain Center where you'll turn east (left) on State Highway 74, the Palms to Pines Highway (or Pines to Palms, depending on your point of view and/or itinerary). This is another official scenic highway and a spectacular descent through several life zones to the floor of the Colorado Desert. It starts at 4,444 feet in Mountain Center, climbs to 4,917 feet at Santa Rosa Summit, and drops to 223 feet at Palm Desert. On the way you'll pass Hurkey Creek County Park, named for some poor fellow who was mauled to death by a grizzly, and Lake Hemet, a pretty mountain lake. Although an eyesore campground near the road is off-putting, continue on the access road to the day-use area and you'll find some nice picnic areas from which to enjoy Lake Hemet. The lake is stocked with fish, but alas, closed to swimming.

The road sweeps through the flat meadowlands of Garner Valley where a gold rush briefly flared in 1890, then begins descending into a luxuriant zone of chaparral. A few yucca spires are harbingers of the desert vegetation just ahead. A side dirt road leads south to Toro Peak (8,716 feet), tallest in the Santa Rosa Range. Be sure to stop at Cahuilla Tewanet Vista Point, which has fine views of the Santa Rosa Mountains to the south. Signs along a short nature walk identify trailside plants and tell how the Cahuilla Indians used them. This palm-pine region was the realm of the Cahuillas and they knew how to harvest its natural bounty for food and medicine: pine nuts, mesquite beans, agave hearts, and oak acorns. They were also masterful basket-makers; some excellent examples are on display in the Palm Springs Desert Museum.

It's time now to get out your parachute for the drop down Seven Level Hill. Bighorn sheep lurk in the rocky side canyons, but those deft recluses are unlikely to show themselves. The road switchbacks through life zones: Upper Sonoran to Transitional Golf Course Zone to Lower Sonoran, with dizzying views of the Coachella Valley. At

Near the bottom of the Palms-to-Pines Highway, an ocotillo signals your arrival in the low desert, with verdant Palm Springs just below.

last it lands you gently on the valley floor, onto State Highway 111 in the town of Palm Desert.

Highway 111 here is no backroad, but you may as well enjoy its 13-mile passage through the glitzy desert resorts. I won't attempt to interpret the entire resort sprawl, but I'll note a few stops worth making that are in keeping with the nature of this tour.

Living Desert

Just to the east of Highway 74 is The Living Desert, a wonderful 1,200-acre desert reserve, museum, zoo, and education center. You can walk or take a tram tour through sectors that re-create life in many of the world's deserts. Taking your time in the Sonoran and Mojave zones will help you identify many of the plants encountered in the tours in this book, plus you'll get to see many of the native critters you're unlikely to encounter in the wild, such as bighorn sheep, mountain lions, rattlesnakes, tortoises, and various raptors.

PALM OASES

Continue toward Palm Springs on Highway 111, East Palm Canyon Drive. Where the road bends sharply to the right, turn left on South Palm Canyon Drive, the road to the famous Indian Canyons—the world's most abundant fan palm oases. The oases belong to the Agua Caliente tribe of the Cahuilla Indians, and the canyons are on reservation land. Five palm canyons flourish here among abundant, flowing water—scenes that seem to be some idealist's interpretation of paradise. Fifteen-mile-long Palm Canyon has more palm trees than any other in the world. A gentle trail departs from the Trading Post, where you can purchase maps, souvenirs, Indian crafts, and cool drinks. Up the West Fork channel of Palm Canyon are some examples of ancient rock art. You can arrange a very informative guided tour of the Indian Canyons and other wild areas near Palm Springs with a group called Desert Adventures (619-864-6530).

DESERT MUSEUM

Back on Highway 111, proceed into central Palm Springs and follow the signs to Palm Springs Desert Museum. The well-endowed museum combines a world-class art collection, the natural history of the desert, and an outstanding anthropology department, primarily representing the local Cahuilla Indians. As I mentioned earlier, the native baskets are superb, and the displays on everyday life of the Cahuilla are fascinating. It's amazing to realize that the natives managed to eke out a living here without a single golf course or fashion boutique to enhance their lives. Some excellent dioramas show the lifestyles of other desert natives: rattlesnakes, gila monsters, kangaroo rats, lizards, and scorpions. And how often do you get to see a seismograph in action? It's interesting to see, but of course you hope not to see *much* action from the machine as it registers the ongoing tremors of the earth. The museum closes at the end of May and reopens in September.

TRAMWAY TO HEAVEN

If you think you can bypass the Palm Springs Aerial Tramway because you've been up a few ski lifts in your day, try it anyway. The Tramway is a stunning accomplishment of engineering, but even better, the painless way to get most of the way up Mount San Jacinto. Take the steep Tramway Road off Highway 111 to the base of the tramway at 2,643 feet. The 80-passenger, cable-operated cars then carry you up another 5,873 vertical feet, high above the sheer sides of Chino Canyon to the upper terminal at 8,516 feet. The ride sweeps above several ecological zones, from lower sonoran

Two cars always meet at the halfway point of the Palm Springs Aerial Tramway between the 2,643-foot Valley Station and the 8,516-foot Mountain Station on Mount San Jacinto.

up to arctic-alpine, in 14 minutes. When it's hot on the desert floor, the air is blessedly cool at the top (the difference is typically 40 degrees). In winter, figure on lots of snow. Many passengers neglect to bring sufficiently warm clothes and end up spending their time inside the mountain station. The view is still awesome, but plan ahead and enjoy the outdoors. Wonderful trails lead from the tramway into the San Jacinto Wilderness. It's 5.5 miles from the station to Mount San Jacinto Peak, at 10,804 feet. In summer you can arrange for a guided mule ride, and in winter you can rent cross-country ski gear to ski in Round Valley.

If you're wondering how the tramway was built, you can watch a hopelessly corny video on the subject in the mountain station. Here's my one-word synopsis: helicopters.

WINDMILL HILLS

When you come down from the mountain and continue on Highway 111 toward I-10, you see windmills. Lots of them. Don Quixote's worse nightmare. No fewer than 4,200

Windmills outside Palm Springs generate electricity for 92,000 Coachella Valley homes. Majestic Mount San Jacinto forms the backdrop.

of the wind turbines stand in the San Gorgonio Pass, one of America's windiest places. As the warm desert air rises, it forms a low-pressure system that literally pulls the cooler coastal air eastward. The wind compresses and increases in speed as it sweeps through the pass. Each windmill needs about an acre of land. As the blades of each turbine spin at speeds of up to 200 mph, they generate electricity which travels through underground cables to a substation. It then travels to high-voltage overhead lines and delivers 544,000 kilowatts annually to some 92,000 homes in the Coachella Valley.

Follow Highway 111 to Interstate 10 west to return to Los Angeles. Or take I-10 briefly east to State Highway 62 to Yucca Valley and pick up Tour 15—or continue to Joshua Tree National Monument and Tour 13.

Julian, Palomar, and the Laguna Mountains

125 Miles
*Mission San Luis Rey • Mount Palomar • Santa Ysabel •
Julian • Cuyamaca Rancho State Park • Laguna
Mountains*

The well-preserved mining town of Julian is the centerpiece of this tour of the mountainous backcountry of San
Diego County, which also takes in other dot-on-the-map
towns and some of the most dramatic, wide-sweeping
viewpoints in Southern California. History here is not just
a matter of ancient echoes, but seems to live on—in the
Spanish missions, Indian reservations, gold-mining ruins,
and a small-town way of life that flourishes so close to metropolitan San Diego.

To begin the tour: From Los Angeles, drive south on
Interstate 5 (Santa Ana Freeway) to Oceanside, and take
State Highway 76 east.

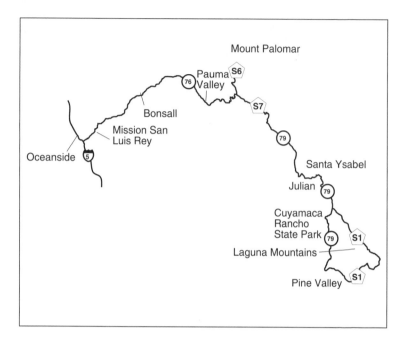

KING OF THE MISSIONS

First stop is Mission San Luis Rey, four miles east of the interstate on Highway 76, called Mission Avenue through Oceanside. As you approach, note the irony of a sign proclaiming "San Luis Rey Historic District" right out in front of a modern-day shopping center replete with fast-food joints. At least it has a Spanish-style red-tile roof. Be patient. Soon you'll see, hovering on a knoll above a sea of mobile homes, the lovely whitewashed mission.

San Luis Rey, "King of the Missions," was founded in 1798 by Fray Fermín de Lasuén and named for St. Louis, 13th-century king of France. Like the other 20 California missions, San Luis Rey had two primary purposes: to Christianize the Indians and to serve as a center of enterprise. Some historians suggest that the goal was less to evangelize than to subdue the natives, and diverting to income-producing labor any energy that might otherwise be spent on hostility toward the colonizing Spaniards. Anyway, some 3,000 Indians served the mission, tending huge herds of sheep and cattle and cultivating large groves of oranges, grapes, and olives.

The mission fell into decay in 1834 when all the missions were secularized. Governor Pio Pico sold San Luis Rey into private hands for $2,500, the natives retreated to the hills, and the mission eventually crumbled. It was none other than President Abraham Lincoln who set in motion the salvation of the mission when he restored the title deed to the Church in 1865. A copy of the document he signed just a month before his assassination is on display in the mission museum.

The restored mission is a classic of the genre, with its open-courtyard gardens, long colonnades, and red-tiled roof. The padres learned what many modern-day Californians haven't—that tile roofs discourage fires, and that thick, buttressed walls withstand earthquakes. (The adobe walls of the mission church are six feet thick.) The mission today is a parish church and retreat center. The museum has some fine historic photos—one poignantly shows a padre and native

San Luis Rey near Oceanside was regarded as "king of the missions." Beautifully restored, the adobe walls of the mission church are six feet thick.

surveying the crumbled mission—and rooms that depict the old mission industries and lifestyle.

TOWARD PALOMAR

You can leave the mission by turning east (left) on Mission Drive, but the more interesting and less developed route is to bear right out of the Mission on Douglas Drive to North River Road, which skirts the San Luis Rey River. The scenery quickly becomes rural, with fields of strawberries, hothouses of tomatoes, and groves of citrus, as well as roadside stands peddling these wares. Business must be good, judging by the grandeur of the farmhouses. North River Road joins Highway 76 in Bonsall (turn left), a little town with a hay-and-grain store on one side and an antique center on the other.

Proceeding east on Highway 76, you'll cross Old Highway 395 and Interstate 15. A fast-food stand here is inexplicably called "Nessy Burgers" in honor of the Loch Ness Monster. Go figure. Beyond the interstate, the road enters a rugged valley with rocky slopes. In its broader segments are a couple of lush, green, oak-shaded horse farms. In its narrower segments it concentrates the olfactory delight of large cattle ranches. Ahead you can see the impressive relief of the Palomar Mountains.

In the little town of Pala, heart of the Pala Indian Reservation, is Mission San Antonio de Pala, built in 1816 as a sort of satellite mission to serve the Indians, which it still does. And yes, the reservation abuts Cleveland National Forest, but no, the Palas are not called the Cleveland Indians.

The town of Pauma Valley, population 876, seems to have a few hundred citrus trees per resident and but one business that bustles—Gilberto's Taco Stand.

Just beyond Pauma Valley, turn north on County Road S6, the steep and winding climb into the pine-covered mountains that include Mount Palomar, which isn't the tallest peak in the range. That honor goes to the prosaically named High Point—6,140 feet. Palomar is easy to spot, of course, crowned as it is by the white-domed Hale Telescope. You'll also spot two smaller domed telescopes. As you climb, you get glimpses of the high peaks to the east, and to the west, a succession of purply silhouettes of lesser ranges that seem to disappear into mist or ocean. Be sure to heed the sign about halfway up that strictly prohibits snowball throwing.

Most of the Palomar range lies in the Cleveland National Forest, but there's also camping and picnicking near the observatory in Mount Palomar State Park. Turn left at the top of the grade on S7 to go to the park. Otherwise, continue on S6 to the observatory.

THE HALE TELESCOPE

You can't view the heavens through the 200-inch Hale Telescope—a privilege left to astronomers from Cal Tech in Pasadena, who mostly view photographs in the control room—but you can view the telescope itself. Jaded as we are by science fiction, this artifact of real science, put into operation in 1948, is still a high-tech marvel to behold. Walk upstairs in the 135-foot dome to see the 200-inch mirror and its 55-foot telescopic tube, plus the mechanisms that drive the 530-ton apparatus with perfect precision and smoothness. It took eight years of meticulous grinding to produce the kind of accuracy required for the mirror, which is so heavy that it actually sags under its own weight. Thirty-six counterbalances support it so it can retain accuracy to a few millionths of an inch when pointed in any direction.

After seeing the telescope, stop in the museum down below to see photos and videos of the Hale at work. It's still an important research site, although growing urbanization has plagued the observatory with light pollution. Displays in the museum address that problem, but also show some remarkable images of distant stars and galaxies. A replica of the 200-inch mirror is also on display.

When you descend from the road that leads to the observatory, you'll return to a saddle and the intersection of county roads S6 and S7. The Corner Store/Cafe here may lure you in with the scent of baking bread. Then turn west (right) on S7 to visit Doane Pond and the camping and picnicking areas of Mount Palomar State Park. Turn left to descend on S7, the East Grade —a longer, gentler road than the way you came up—and rejoin Highway 76 at Lake Henshaw.

APPROACH TO JULIAN

Lake Henshaw rests at the west edge of a huge round plateau that's ringed by forests, but the lake is curiously devoid of vegetation and looks a little forlorn out there in the open. Highway 76 ends a few miles later at Morettis Junction. Turn right on Highway 79 and follow it through the verdant valley of Santa Ysabel Creek to the town of Santa Ysabel. Once again, the scent of baking bread dough may lure you out of the car. Dudley's Bakery has been a Santa Ysabel institution since 1963. Although it's a huge bakery and its breads are popular county-wide, Dudley's has a friendly, small-town atmosphere. Very Mom-like ladies bake the bread, run the counter, and serve up samples.

Just up the road in Wynola is another local institution, Tom's Chicken Shack, as well as a fine produce market. The surrounding apple trees hint at a Wynola/Julian specialty: apple pie. You can follow the scent of baking pie right on into Julian, or for a gorgeous backroad approach, turn left on Wynola Road and follow it to Highway 78 and into Julian. This very narrow, winding two-laner slices through oak and pine forests and serves up occasional glimpses of the Christmas tree farms, apple orchards, and ranches of backcountry Julian.

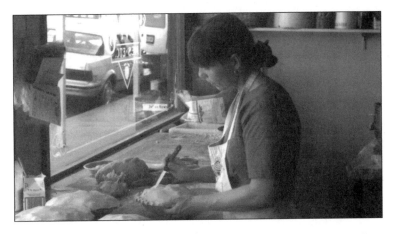

Main Street Julian is redolent with the scent of apple pies baking. Here a baker at Mom's readies a fresh batch.

JULIAN

It doesn't take long to get acquainted with downtown Julian, but it's a delightful acquaintance to nurture. Julian is certainly one of Southern California's most pleasant weekend destinations. Rustic, woodsy, and just a few blocks long, it has managed to retain a strong sense of its origins as an 1880s gold town. Not a boom town, mind you. That Julian never was. It was never one of those supernova cities crawling with bars and brothels. Gold-panners first found gold in a creek near the site of Julian in 1869. A year later, prospectors found a quartz ledge they presumed to be the source of the placer gold, and on Washington's Birthday, 1870, opened the Washington Mine. One of those prospectors, a former Confederate soldier named Drue Bailey, applied for a 160-acre homestead patent that included the site of the present-day town. He didn't receive it until 1888. When he did, he called the town Julian City in honor of his friend and fellow Confederate prospector, Mike Julian. Mike was better looking than he, Drue explained.

Prospectors eventually made Swiss cheese of the mountain just above the town, but Julian's gold finds were never wildly lucrative. Mining continued until the early 1930s, but the total for the entire region during 60 years of mining was under $4 million. One mine remains open—the Eagle, near the original Washington. No one mines it, but they will take you for a tour through two long shafts on two levels. Walk or drive six blocks up C Street to the 1870 mine. It's sobering to see what hard work hard-rock mining was; most of the mine was dug by hand, before power tools or explosives. At the end of the tour, the guide will let you try your hand at gold-panning.

Truth is, apples have been more lucrative than gold for Julian, and the place resembles a boom town on fall weekends, when the apple harvest and crisp weather lure city folks up in droves. But you're well served any time you visit Julian. Every dining establishment in town save one

The 1887 Julian Hotel was built by a freed slave. A Victorian atmosphere prevails in the 18-room inn, one of many charming bed-and-breakfasts in Julian.

(the Italian restaurant stays out of the fray) dishes up Julian apple pie, characterized by homemade crust and crisp apples—not too sweet, but richly spiced.

Behind the rustic edifices of downtown Julian are good restaurants (the Julian Grille stands out), antique and gift shops, and a historical museum open on weekends only. The most striking building in town is the Julian Hotel, established in 1887 by former slave Albert Robinson. The hotel is today a bed-and-breakfast inn, authentically furnished with antiques and presenting a cozy, genteel ambience. Julian being a bed-and-breakfast kind of place, you'll also find several other country inns in and around town.

CUYAMACA RANCHO

The mountain peaks and pristine valleys of Cuyamaca Rancho State Park, just south of Julian on Highway 79, were once part of a grant deeded in 1845 to Agustin Olvera by Mexican Governor Pio Pico. Olvera's plan to harvest timber from the Cuyamaca forests fizzled in the face of resistance from local Indians. Only when gold was discovered in the northern part of the rancho did the area attract much interest. Funny how that works.

Highway 79 leads through the piney northern reaches of the Cuyamaca Mountains and deposits you on the shores of Lake Cuyamaca. Behind it looms the distinctive hulk of Stonewall Peak. The lake's claim to fame today is as a decent fishing hole yielding some good-size bass and trout. But it was once a critical water source for eastern San Diego and part of an interesting footnote to California's tempestuous water history. The dam was built in 1889 to store water—but how to get it to San Diego? Simple. Hire a lot of Chinese labor and build a flume. The amazing, all-wood Cuyamaca Flume carried water 36 miles to its terminus a few miles east of San Diego. It was constructed during two years of intensive labor from nine billion board feet of clear-heart redwood planks. It had to be graded precisely while passing over high trestles and through solid rock mountains. By 1919, The Flume was rendered redundant by larger reservoirs. Few traces of The Flume project remain but for the dam at Cuyamaca.

Just beyond the lake is a turnoff for Stonewall Mine. This was by far the best-producing gold mine in the Julian area. From 1872 to 1892, it produced over $2 million worth of gold. Like many other mines in the area, it was claimed by former Confederate soldiers. They named it Stonewall Jackson mine, but later amended the name to Stonewall Mine so as not to offend potential Yankee investors. Some stone ruins remain today, imprisoned by a state park fence.

Cuyamaca Rancho became a state park in 1933, and its sprawling 26,000 acres contain some wonderful hiking trails. One leads 3.5 miles to the top of Cuyamaca Peak (6,512 feet), where a rewarding view extends to the Pacific and to Mexico. A gentler trail passes through Azalea Glen in Paso Picacho Campground. When the trail emerges from a pine-oak forest (you'll walk by one particularly massive canyon oak) into an open meadow, you can see some low

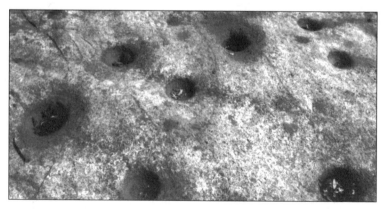

These bedrock mortars, known as morteros, *were created by native women grinding acorns into flour. These are along the Azalea Glen Trail in Cuyamaca Rancho State Park.*

granite boulders pocked with potholes. These bedrock mortars were created by Indian women grinding acorns. (As you'll see, there was certainly no shortage of acorns.) The flavor of raw acorns is bitter, full of face-twisting tannins. To render them edible, the women ground them into flour using stone or oak-wood pestles, then spent many hours leaching the flour of tannins. Only then could the flour be used for baking or cooked into a mush.

Continuing south on Highway 79 from Paso Picacho, you'll descend to Green Valley and soon come to the turnoff for the park headquarters and interpretive center, standing in a dark forest of black oak, coast live oak, and pine trees. Notice the beautifully constructed stone arch bridge as you cross over Sweetwater River. Park headquarters is in a grand old stone house, with native oak beams inside, originally built as a vacation home by a wealthy San Diegan. Inside, the interpretive center has exhibits on local Indian life, including some outstanding examples of native basketry.

After park headquarters, Highway 79 descends from the pine-covered Cuyamacas to smaller-scale hills cloaked with chaparral. Chaparral, the scrub-oak brush that is one of Southern California's trademark landscapes, always loves sandstone hills. Among the sandstone peaks and projections are a number of houses built to blend in with the ambience; many are so camouflaged you can barely see them.

OLD HIGHWAY 80

Outside the park's southern gate, you'll come to a junction. The general store here sells Dudley's breads, just in case you've run through the loaf you bought in Santa Ysabel. Turn left, then left again on Old Highway 80 toward Guatay and Pine Valley. Interstate 8 swallowed up most of the old highway, but this stretch is a remnant, and like most bypassed old routes, it's pretty sleepy. Guatay seems at first to be but a cluster of mobile homes and a cafe among huge oaks. But a bit further along is "downtown," where there's a hardware store, a market, and a lot of shacks landscaped the old-fashioned way—with rusting car parts, farm implements, and used tires. Two diamonds lurk in this rough: an herb shop called Earth Emporium (it feels salubrious just to walk inside and breathe deeply) and a gallery of wood carvings called Tryyn. The word is old English for "of the tree." The specialty of carver William V. Chappelow is wooden spoons whittled from all manner of exotic woods into whimsical shapes—worth a look if not a purchase for a striking gift or keepsake. Chappelow's spoons have found their way to the Smithsonian and to galleries, collectors, and yes, to kitchens, all over the country. Down the road, Pine Valley is a sleepy, shady little town, a bit larger than Guatay, with cafes and motels.

LAGUNA MOUNTAINS

At the outskirts of Pine Valley, where you could turn right to join Interstate 8, turn left instead on County Road S1, also known as Sunrise Highway. Sunrise is an official Forest Service Scenic Byway, and scenic it is. As it heads north and climbs into Cleveland National Forest, it passes through arid hills dense with fluffy green pinyons and twisted manzanita. At 5,000 feet, you're in the Laguna Mountains among tall pine trees, and it becomes cool and shady. A number of campgrounds and picnic areas here are popular with flatlanders looking to cool off in summer or to play in occasional snow in winter.

The Lagunas are one of those desert-fringe ranges that soak up whatever moisture is left in the clouds passing inland from the coast, creating the rain shadow that makes Anza-Borrego Desert a desert. The phenomenon is obvious if you stop at one of the east-looking viewpoints. Desert View picnic area is one. Or better, turn right at the sign that says "Vista Point" and follow the road out onto a ridge to the base of two old fenced-off Air Force radar domes. From this high vantage (about 6,000 feet), you can see the raw, ash-gray peaks and flatlands of the desert, criss-crossed with mysterious-looking trails.

Sunrise Highway continues along the eastern flank of the Lagunas with more desert views, and if you look carefully, views to the north of Mounts San Gorgonio and San Jacinto, the distant, tallest peaks of Southern California. The road then retreats to the west, forsaking the Lagunas and returning to the wide pastures that surround Lake Cuyamaca. Turn right and retrace your way six miles back into Julian.

From here, you can follow Highway 78 out of Julian toward Escondido. This is a very pretty route that passes through several fertile valleys before it becomes freeway in Escondido and rejoins I-5. Just east of Escondido is the San Diego Wild Animal Park, where you can take a monorail or truck tour and view exotic animals roaming uncaged in habitats that more or less resemble their native landscapes. Or you can follow Highway 79 north to County Roads 2 and 22—San Felipe and Montezuma Valley Roads—and into Anza-Borrego Desert State Park, described in Tour 16.

TOUR 10

The Ojai and Cuyama Valleys

155 miles
Ojai • Scenic Highway 33 • Wheeler Gorge • Cuyama Valley • Santa Maria

Shangri-La being a fictional paradise, many locales lay claim to being a Shangri-La of some sort, but few can boast as legitimately as Ojai. After all, Hollywood accorded it the Shangri-La mantle (and that swings a lot of weight in Southern California) by filming part of the original, 1937 *Lost Horizon* in the Ojai Valley. It's a place of great appeal with a stunning setting, but it's only the start of this tour, which leads out of Ojai into its backcountry and then finds wide-open farmland in a forgotten valley.

To begin the tour: Take U.S. Highway 101, the Ventura Freeway, west to Ventura, then take State Highway 33 north toward Ojai.

Highway 33 begins along the light-industrial backside of Ventura as it leads through the wide valley of the Ventura River. In spring, fields of mustard form skirts for the sandstone-tufted crests that frame the valley. After a few miles, the

110

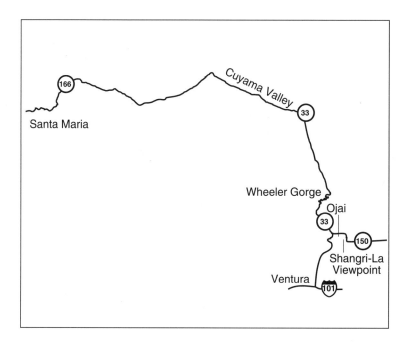

road narrows to two lanes, a bike path appears on the left, and tall eucalyptus trees elegantly line the approach to Ojai.

First you'll pass through a couple of hamlets, Casitas Springs and Oak View, which, with their bait shops, fruit stands, and antique shops, are considerably less precious than Ojai. At the junction with State Highway 150, turn right. The prestigious prep schools and the Ojai Valley Inn and Country Club are a tip-off: Ojai is a very different world.

NEST OR MOON?

"Ojai" is a Chumash Indian word, but there's disagreement as to its meaning. Some say it's "nest," others say "moon." Unfortunately, there aren't many Chumash around to settle the matter. They lived in the valley and ranged the Southern California coast for hundreds of years until the Spaniards arrived to "save" them. The Spaniards put the natives to work on their missions and introduced them to such exotic wonders as tuberculosis and measles. Few of them survived into the 20th century.

In 1872, an itinerant journalist named Charles Nordhoff published a book about California and particularly extolled the Ojai Valley—its climate, mineral baths, and natural setting. Nordhoff's book and magazine articles were widely read in the east. The place soon became a magnet for tourists and farmers, and the town took the name "Nordhoff." The name reverted to Ojai in 1917—German-sounding names were not in vogue during World War I.

DOWNTOWN

On one side of Ojai Avenue, as Highway 150 is known through town, a row of arcaded boutiques sell things like "wearable art," Indian jewelry, pottery, and gourmet food items, while courtyard cafes provide relaxed settings for savoring cappucino and muffins or tea and scones. On the other side, a graceful, Spanish-style tower above the Post Office stands as the landmark building of Ojai, and Libbey Park, site of Ojai's annual late-spring music festival, has a fantasy playground for children—a peaceful, natural setting in the heart of downtown. Of course, the whole town is in a peaceful, natural setting, with the escarpment known as Topa Topa Ridge providing a dramatic backdrop to the north. The Sulphur Mountains to the south form the other piece of the valley frame. Locals speak of "pink time" in Ojai, when Topa Topa Ridge catches a rosy alpenglow from the setting sun.

Be sure to explore the side streets of Ojai, where you'll find more cafes, shops, and hidden treasures like Bart's Books (one block north of Ojai Avenue, at the corner of Canada and Matilija). Bart's might be the world's only outdoor bookstore. Actually, part of it is inside an old house,

Downtown arcade and the Post Office Tower are landmarks of Ojai, a town that invites strolling and browsing.

but all around it, on an oak-shaded patio and even out on the sidewalk, are shelf after shelf containing 100,000 used books. South of Ojai Avenue, you can walk down Montgomery Street to the Ojai Valley Museum and a block farther to a bike path that leads through town and follows Highway 33 toward the ocean.

Ojai draws a lot of well-heeled tourists, so naturally, it has some fine places to eat. One of note is the Ranch House, one of the most romantic restaurants anywhere. Diners sit inside what feels like a gracious ranch house or on the patio beside the garden. The recipes are always creative and always use herbs grown in the garden as well as local produce, and the home-baked bread and desserts are always delicious. It's a special and tranquil place.

UPPER OJAI VALLEY

Ojai's serene beauty has long attracted artists, musicians, and spiritualists, among them the late Indian philosopher

Jiddu Krishnamurti. A number of holistic healing and teaching centers are in and around Ojai, including the Krishnamurti Library.

Ojai's most famous artist is the remarkable ceramist Beatrice Wood, who was 101 at the time of this writing, still highly productive, and still given to saying things like, "Celibacy is exhausting." Her studio is east of town off Highway 150. She welcomes visitors—indeed, assents to being listed as a "Point of Interest" in local tourism publications. To get there, take Highway 150 east past large citrus groves and up the switchbacks known as Dennison Grade to Upper Ojai Valley. On the way, pull over at the signed viewpoint to look down on Shangri-La. This was the view that the Ronald Colman character beheld as paradise in the movie *Lost Horizon*.

Once you're in upper Ojai Valley, which is just as beautiful as the valley below (and utterly undeveloped), look for a pink mailbox and a sign for Happy Valley School and Beatrice Wood Studio. The studio is in her hilltop home surrounded by an ornate cactus garden.

Upper Ojai Valley is a Shangri-La in itself, a pastoral version of the Ojai Valley that served as paradise in the original Lost Horizon.

Inside, if Ms. Wood is up to greeting visitors (she usually is between 1 and 5 p.m.) you will get to meet a living treasure. Her eyes sparkle like her wit, and she betrays a fondness for chocolate and young men. Her art is exquisite, from complex, iridescently gleaming bowls and chalices, to comical, folk-art "naughty figures." It's amazing to realize that this wonderful artist, whose work graces galleries and homes worldwide, who has been featured on public radio and television, was also a leading figure in the Dada art scene before World War I.

UP THE MATILIJA

When you've finished exploring Ojai, return to Highway 33 and turn north toward the mountains. You'll soon be in the canyon of Matilija Creek. In May and June, watch for the tall, elegant, white-petaled matilija poppy beside the road—the flowers are four to five inches in diameter and blossom from bushes as tall as seven feet. About six miles above Ojai, you'll come to the Wheeler Hot Springs spa, a Shangri-La in its own right nestled in the dense oak woods, where you can soak in private tubs filled with naturally hot mineral water, indulge in a massage, and polish off the experience with a fine creekside meal.

Beyond the hot springs, the canyon narrows, and the road passes through a series of tunnels before emerging into the sheer rock enclosure of Wheeler Gorge. You're now in the Los Padres National Forest, and a campground and picnic area here give access to the north fork of Matilija Creek, cool and shaded with tall cottonwoods.

The road soon starts sweeping up and out of the gorge, leaving behind the dark oak valley for the realm of chaparral. In spring, a sea of blue-tufted ceanothus blossoms brighten the generally drab shrubs, while lupine and bright yellow broom line the road cuts.

*Matilija Creek burbles
alongside Highway 33 north
of Ojai.*

Near the top of the climb is a cutoff for Rose Valley, a six-mile side trip to several national forest campgrounds tucked away in this mountainous backcountry. From Middle Lion Campground you can hike along Sespe Creek into the Sespe Wilderness, a place local activists have fought hard to preserve (staving off pressure to dam the stream to allow more development down below). Cool pools in the Sespe, framed by huge boulders, make great swimming holes. This is also the area where wildlife biologists have been trying to reintroduce into the wild the nearly extinct California condor.

Continuing on Highway 33, you soon reach the road's crest. Pull over and gaze down into the valley of the Matilija and Ventura Rivers and you can see your entire journey to this point unfold below you. Ridges and subranges of the Topa Topa and Santa Ynez Mountains dip down to the

Pacific, and then there's another range. How's that? Well, from this perspective, the Channel Islands, 12 to 15 miles offshore, look like yet another upthrust of coastal mountain. From here the road heads into a valley, following a non-wilderness stretch of Sespe Creek. Just above is the Pine Mountain massif, topped by Reyes Peak at 7,510 feet. A steep sandstone escarpment, pocked with erosion nooks and holes, gazes down on the road—an eerie touch to a wild, remote stretch of backroad. It's a perfect setting for Pine Mountain Inn, a roadhouse bar and grill. Duck inside and you'll see autographed dollar bills tacked to every available wall and ceiling surface. It seems that someone, years ago, tacked up a buck in case he was short the next time he came in for a drink. The custom caught on.

A few miles beyond the inn is a side road that leads to national forest campgrounds and a trailhead for the short climb to Reyes Peak. Finally, Highway 33 reaches its apex at Pine Mountain Summit (5,084 feet). A panoramic view reveals the route we'll be taking through the green fields of Cuyama Valley and beyond, where you can see the Utah-style, red-rock Cuyama Badlands.

CUYAMA VALLEY

Highway 33 now descends into the valley of the Cuyama River, one of those now-you-see-it, now-you-don't California rivers. Even where the bed is dry and sandy, extensive farms that fill this remote valley suggest the presence of a lot of underground water. Carrots are the root of Cuyama Valley agriculture.

Turn left at the junction of State Highway 166 and continue following the course of the Cuyama River to the twin cities of Cuyama (population 162) and New Cuyama (population 1,100). Cuyama has a post office approximately the size of a shoe box, plus a grocery store and a feed store made of corrugated tin. By contrast, New Cuyama is a

The pace is unhurried and life unfettered among the farms and ranches of Cuyama Valley.

bustling metropolis. Few towns in Southern California feel more removed in time and space than the Cuyamas, and even fewer serve up ostrich burgers, as does the Buckhorn Restaurant in New Cuyama. In case you've had your head in the sand and hadn't heard, ostriches yield a tasty red meat that's leaner than beef.

Highway 166 crosses and flirts with the Cuyama River now, and the spine of the Sierra Madre Mountains draws closer until finally the highway bisects the mountains. Impressive sandstone formations hover above as the road begins a long descent of the Sierra Madre foothills. This is classic California *potrero* country—rolling, cattle-ranch hills of wild oats, green in spring, golden the rest of the year—studded with small spots of coast live oak on the hillsides and vast, dark groves in the canyons. As the highway undulates alongside Twitchell Reservoir, which is as mercurial as the Cuyama River that fills it at times, a glimmer of ocean ahead indicates the end of this backroad journey. You'll soon come to the junction of U.S. Highway 101 just north of Santa Maria. From here you can head south to Los Alamos or to the Santa Ynez Valley and pick up Tour 2 or 3.

TOUR 11

Temecula Valley: A Taste of Old California

76 miles
Santa Rosa Plateau Reserve • Old Town Temecula •
Temecula Wine Country • Lake Skinner • De Luz •
Fallbrook

It's always exciting to come upon vestiges of old California. Whether these are places where nearly extinct native plants and trees still grow or backwoods settlements where old ways of life flourish, it's refreshing to know that progress hasn't obliterated values and landscapes that once defined the promised land of Southern California.

This tour through part of the so-called Inland Empire and on into rural San Diego County is a tour of such vestiges, linked together by untrodden backroads. It's a short tour worth taking for the pure pleasure of the drive, but there's also plenty along the way to urge you out of the car.

To begin the tour: Take State Highway 60 (Pomona Freeway) or Interstate 10 (Santa Monica Freeway) east from Los Angeles to Interstate 15. Take I-15 south to the Clinton Keith Road exit in Murrieta. Proceed south (right) on Clinton Keith Road.

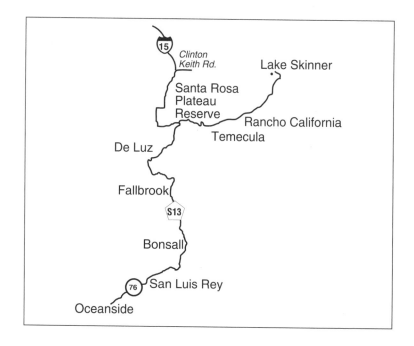

SANTA ROSA PLATEAU

Clinton Keith Road hurries you past a few modern sub-divisions and into the open countryside of the Santa Rosa Plateau, a place of rolling hills at the southern end of the Santa Ana Mountains. Happily, Nature Conservancy manages a huge preserve here that is little changed since the days of huge ranchos and Mexican land grants. After five miles you'll come to the first entrance to the Santa Rosa Plateau Ecological Preserve.

The road skirts the western edge of the preserve and offers good views of the rolling grasslands, flat-topped mesas, and oak woodlands. The preserve is the best bastion of the grand Engelmann oak. Oak aficionados appreciate the way the branches spread, contort, and dip gracefully to the savannah floor—even more gnarled and angular than the coast live oak. These are the most endangered of California oaks and the stands in the Santa Rosa Plateau are the best remaining Engelmanns anywhere.

The Santa Rosa Plateau also contains rare vernal pools—depressions in ancient volcanic flows of basalt that hold rainwater long into spring, then recede slowly, leaving concentric rings of colorful wildflowers. And the plateau preserves native bunchgrasses, once the standard groundcover in California but obliterated by Spanish-introduced wild oats and barley. It's a moving experience to stand in the plateau, with its broad, unfettered horizons, amid prairies of bunchgrass (easy to recognize—it grows in clumps) and wide-spreading Engelmann oaks.

The first stop in the preserve is the trailhead for the Granite Loop and Vista Grande hikes—both short ones that give a good taste of the high, boulder-strewn plateau and fine views of prairies and woodlands. It also leads across several *tenajas* (seasonal streams) full of frogs and turtles.

Stately Englemann oaks are the largest and most endangered of California oaks. Many of the trees, as well as rare native grasses and vernal pools, are found in the Santa Rosa Plateau Preserve.

The second trailhead, a few miles down the road, is the best stop for oak-viewing. A fine, 350-year-old Engelmann stands at the head of a trail that leads through one of the very last groves of self-reproducing Engelmanns. And the third stop leads to several vernal pools (a couple are visible from the road). Along each walk are some of the more showy of Southern California wildflowers: johnny jump-up, shooting star, checkerbloom, and Mariposa lily.

It takes but a short walk onto the plateau to enter its serene world filled with sounds of songbirds. It feels familiar and strange at the same time—an endemic landscape that has been rendered a rarity.

Back on the road, simply follow your nose as you skirt the preserve boundary traveling counterclockwise. The road changes names a few times. As Los Gatos Road, it drops steeply off the plateau and into hill country and avocado ranches. Turn left on Carancho, left on De Luz and right on Rancho California. High up on Rancho California Road, you'll get a huge aerial view of the Temecula Valley before the road plops you into the town of Temecula.

OLD TOWN TEMECULA

Much of Temecula is burgeoning suburbia, but Old Town Temecula preserves a bit of Old California—with a few nods to new tourism. When you come into town on Rancho California, turn right (south) on Front Street (a remnant of Old Highway 395) and continue to the corner of Main Street, the heart of Old Town.

Be sure to stop in the Temecula Museum on Main Street, which harbors a few surprises. In addition to historical displays and Indian exhibits, there's a mysterious ancient stone carving of a human face found in an area where the native Indians were hunters, farmers, and basketweavers—but not stone carvers. Another novelty is the Erle Stanley

Antiques are the biggest lure to Old Town Temecula. The mural on the side of Temecula Trading Post commemorates the Butterfield Overland Stage. Coaches passed through Temecula on their way from Missouri to Monterey.

Gardner exhibit; the *Perry Mason* author lived in Temecula from 1937 until his death in 1970.

Temecula first grew as a stage stop on the Butterfield Overland Stage route from St. Louis to San Francisco, then later as a rail stop and the center of Walter Vail's vast cattle empire. It wasn't until the Vail Ranch was sold to developers in 1964, though, that the modern town began to grow.

Old Town is full of historical buildings and antique markets. It doesn't take much imagination to see dusty streets, carriages, and hitching posts in front of the old buildings. The 1914 bank building (which Walter Vail called "my pawn shop") at the corner of Main and Front was the first poured cement building in inland California. Today it's a Mexican restaurant. Around the corner on Main Street are several more old buildings: The Temecula Trading Post is an antique market, and the 1891 Temecula Mercantile, which supplied local ranchers for over 60 years, is an antique mall that

Inside the Chaparral Antique Mall in Old Town Temecula, a number of dealers show their wares in a labyrinthine building.

retains the feeling of a get-anything-you-want place. Several other antique malls and shops face Front Street, some in newer buildings with a faux Old West look. One of these, the labyrinthine Chaparral Antique Mall at the north end of Front Street, houses more than 70 dealers.

WINE COUNTRY

Temecula Valley has lately become one of Southern California's prime grape-growing and wine-producing regions. Thank goodness someone recognized that the hills and valleys east of town could grow something besides stucco. To tour the Temecula wineries, head back up Front Street, turn right (east) on Rancho California, and continue beyond the sprawling tracts of homes. A dozen or so wineries and more than 3,000 acres of grapes line this country road. Most of the wineries offer tastings and tours. The largest is Callaway, which has a pleasant picnic area. Across

*Callaway Winery is the largest of the Temecula Valley wineries and a
fine stop for wine tasting and picnicking.*

the street, Thornton features sparkling wines and the lovely Cafe Champagne with shaded outdoor dining.

You can wine-hop all the way out Rancho California
Road to Lake Skinner, a man-made lake with good trout
and catfish fishing, camping, picnicking, and wilderness
hiking trails. Speedboats are banned here, so the lake is reasonably tranquil.

DE LUZ ROAD

The next leg of this tour is a seriously rural drive through
ranch country and rugged oak hills. Make an about-face on
Rancho California Road and follow it all the way back
through Temecula, up the steep hill where Walter Vail's cattle used to graze (supplanted by scattered mansions), and
left on De Luz Murrieta Road.

De Luz Murrieta Road is a backroads-lover's dream—a
twisting route through deep oak woodlands and rustic old
ranches. It's definitely not the way a crow would fly to
Fallbrook. Take it slow and enjoy the views of the Santa

Margarita Mountains on the west side of the road—the wild, undeveloped back side of Camp Pendleton Marine Base. This old road doesn't bother with niceties like bridges; you just drive through the water (almost always shallow) at stream crossings.

After about 10 miles of ups and downs, twists and turns, watch for a sign: Catwalker Gallery. If it's open, and it usually is on weekends, you're in for a treat. The gallery is part of an old De Luz Canyon ranch, shaded by huge oaks and crossed by a stony brook. If the day is cool, a fire will be burning inside, and gallery owner Jeanette Roll will welcome you in. Inside are jewelry, baskets, ceramics, and decorated gourds. A sign says that all the crafts are made by De Luz residents. Turns out that most of them are made by Jeanette, her husband, and her daughter.

De Luz still shows up on some maps as a settlement, but today it's really just widely scattered ranches. It never really had anything like a village or a downtown, but it did have a school and a post office, both of which are just down the road from the Catwalker. The old De Luz one-room schoolhouse served De Luz children from 1926 to 1968. It's now an environmental education center for the Fallbrook

Tiny De Luz Post Office is a reminder of the old days, which really haven't changed much, along the backroad from Temecula to Fallbrook.

school district. Beside the school, looking a bit like a play-house, is the old post office, which might have been the smallest in the country. The 8' x 8' white wood frame building was built in 1916 and had all of 33 post boxes. Still, it was a mustering point for the dispersed residents of De Luz awaiting the thrice-weekly postal deliveries.

FALLBROOK

Beyond De Luz, the countryside opens out a bit into bulky hills covered with avocado groves. The road makes an impressive drop down to the Margarita River, then climbs back up to the rural town of Fallbrook. Although Fallbrook has plenty of modern amenities, it does retain a country charm—partly because it lies several miles away from Interstate 15, so one doesn't drive through it on the way to anywhere, and partly because it spreads out over 127 square miles, leaving plenty of open space, oak trees, avocado groves, and citrus orchards between homes and shopping centers.

Fallbrook is the kind of place where produce stands pop up whenever a local crop comes into season and antique shops invite casual browsing. To poke around town a bit, turn onto Main Street, where you'll find buildings of nine-teenth-century vintage, antique shops, a coffee house, a bookstore, and places to eat. The Chamber of Commerce on this street can steer you to more antique shops, which abound in and around Fallbrook. Then proceed south on Mission Road (County Road S13), which passes by several more antique shops as it heads out of town, descending toward the valley of San Luis Rey River. Turn right on State Highway 76 and follow it toward Mission San Luis Rey, Oceanside and Interstate 5 back to Los Angeles. Or you can turn left on Highway 76 toward Pala and Mount Palomar and join Tour 9 in progress.

TOUR 12

Rural Orange County and the Santa Ana Mountains

90 miles
*Santiago Oaks Park • Irvine Park • Irvine Lake •
Silverado Canyon • Modjeska Canyon • O'Neill Park •
Trabuco Canyon • Ortega Highway • El Cariso • Lake
Elsinore*

"Rural Orange County" sounds like a joke or an oxy-moron here in the realm of Disney and indiscriminate development. Although the county that so willingly denuded itself of its eponymous citrus long ago still has a penchant for slapping stucco over every available remnant of nature, the vestiges of rural life and unsullied nature that have escaped the bulldozer are almost poignantly alluring. And yes, genuinely rural.

Orange County's eastern flank, you see, is guarded by Cleveland National Forest, which encompasses the Santa Ana Mountains. The Santa Anas are real mountains, not concrete concoctions Swiss-cheesed by thrill rides, and the snow that dusts Santiago and Modjeska Peaks in winter comes from the sky, not a paint can. This tour takes in a foothill road that parallels the range, a couple of time-for-gotten canyon roads that slice into its western edge, and the scenic Ortega Highway, the only road that crosses the range.

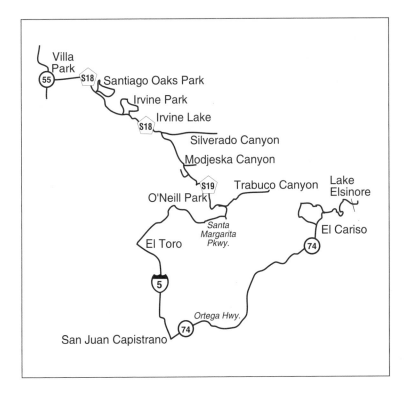

To begin the tour: From Los Angeles, take Interstate 5 (the Santa Ana Freeway) south to State Highway 91 (Riverside Freeway), then go east to State Highway 55 (Costa Mesa Freeway) South. Exit at Katella Avenue and turn left.

SANTIAGO AND THE PARKS

After an unpromising start through suburban Villa Park, our road changes names and character, becoming Santiago Canyon Road (County Road S18), a fast rural road that skirts the foothill fringe of the Santa Ana Mountains. If it seems pretty busy for a backroad, understand that it's the best Orange County has. Everyone's out cruising it, bicy-cling it, or Harley-ing it on a pleasant weekend day.

The early stretch is a bit schizo—nouvelle suburbs next to venerable horse farms. Some bends reveal views of the grassy hills that march into the Santa Ana Mountains, other views show the ominous approach of red-tile roofs. After a little jog to the right on Jamboree and then left to continue with Santiago Canyon, the road's rural nature prevails.

Hikers and equestrians have two opportunities along here to stretch some legs: Santiago Oaks and Irvine Regional Parks. Santiago Oaks has a couple of short walks along Santiago Creek and into the grassy hills. Irvine Park encompasses 447 acres. It's a popular place on summer weekends, but visit in winter or on a weekday and you'll have a lot of serene scenery to yourself, including some giant oaks and a small lagoon. Rancher James Irvine donated the first 160 acres to the county in 1897—a welcome gift, but a mere dollop of the 115,000 acres that made up his spread.

Four miles down the road from Irvine Regional Park is Irvine Lake, also known as Santiago Reservoir. The lake is in private hands and extracts a hefty entrance fee, but the fishing is supposed to be good, particularly for monstrous catfish and rainbow trout.

Santiago Canyon Road now skirts Limestone and Santiago creeks in which you're unlikely to see much water, but an abundance of sycamores and riparian greenery indicates the course of the streams.

SILVERADO CANYON

Shortly past Irvine Lake, turn left on Silverado Canyon Road. Before Walt Disney came along in the 1950s, Silverado Canyon was the site of Orange County's most exciting episode. The canyon was known as Canada de la Madera (canyon of the timber) in the fall of 1877, when two prospectors found a vein of translucent quartz ore that contained a hint of silver. They staked a couple of claims, word of which immediately leaked out. The state had been lousy with prospectors since 1848, and they descended like vermin on the quiet Orange County canyon. In just a few days, another 500 claims were staked and the boom town (camp, really) of Silverado spontaneously erupted.

Other prospectors found coal in the canyon, and a second camp formed, this one more prosaically known as Carbondale. The population of the canyon reached over 1,000. Stagecoaches arrived twice daily from Los Angeles and three times daily from nearby Santa Ana. Stores and saloons sprang up. But the excitement didn't last long. The coal ledges and quartz veins petered out, and by 1883, both towns had gone from boom to ghost.

Folks began returning to the canyon around the time of World War I, some occupying the old camp shacks. Today, Silverado is a rural community with a country store, post office, library, and a couple of restaurants. (Notice that one small side street is cleverly called Thisa Way.) A jumble of homes lines Silverado Creek—some are cobbled together country shacks, some have stone facades, and some are yuppie-era anomalies.

Oak trees drape Silverado Canyon Road as it winds toward the foothills in a rare rural nook of Orange County.

A country store in Orange County would seem anachronistic or staged by Disney, but in rural Silverado Canyon, it's just part of daily life.

As Silverado slices into the Santa Anas, canyon walls loom cozily above the 5.5-mile road. A canopy of oaks hangs over much of the road, and alders, bay laurels, and sycamores line the creek and shade the homes. Apart from the narrow road corridor, the canyon is part of Cleveland National Forest. A ranger station is there primarily to monitor fire conditions but will sell you a forest map and give you information about hiking beyond road's end.

A monument to Silverado and Carbondale marks the end of the road, where there's a turnaround and small parking area. A locked gate marks the entrance to Cleveland National Forest. Park here for an easy stroll along the shady canyon bottom. You can also continue up a more exposed route to Bedford Peak (3,800 feet), a 6.6-mile round trip.

MODJESKA CANYON

After returning to Santiago Canyon Road, continue three miles south and turn up Modjeska Canyon Road, a shorter road with a different flavor and history from its neighbor to the north. Modjeska Canyon takes its name from Polish actress Helena Modjeska (1840–1909), one of the most popular and acclaimed stars of her era. Modjeska and her husband, Count Karol Bozenta Chlapowski, settled a rural enclave here in the 1870s. Joined by other Polish writers and artists, they had a utopian commune of sorts, shocking as such a legacy might seem for staid Orange County. With her great success on the American stage, Madame Modjeska was able to commission a dream home in the foothill canyon. The elegant, gabled home was designed by architect Stanford White and became the centerpiece of a lovely estate its owner called The Forest of Arden, after the Arden of Shakespeare's *As You Like It*. For nearly 20 years, it was the focus of intellectual and artistic life in Orange County.

Life in Modjeska Canyon today isn't quite so glamorous, but the canyon retains a sense of community, with a number of lovely homes scattered among huge, draping oaks. Across from the fire station, you'll spot a plaque commemorating Madame Modjeska, "the woman who contributed immeasurably to the cultural life of Orange County." The home itself is difficult to see behind the thick tangle of oaks and shade trees (it's catty-corner to the fire station), but you can arrange a tour by contacting Heritage Hill Historic Park in Lake Forest: 714-855-2028.

At the head of Modjeska Canyon you'll find Tucker Wildlife Sanctuary, a cool shady spot best known for the several species of hummingbird that flit around here in fairly remarkable numbers. You can sit on an observation porch that overlooks a dozen or so feeders and watch the action, or stroll along short nature trails that interpret the native chaparral. In addition to the hummingbirds, nearly 200 other species of birds have been spotted here. The sanctuary is also the trailhead for a pleasant hike up Harding Trail to Laurel Spring, a 10-mile round trip.

The tallest peaks in the Santa Ana Mountains stand above Modjeska Canyon and dominate views in this area—

Modjeska Peak (5,496 feet) and Santiago Peak (5,687 feet), which together are known as Old Saddleback. These peaks are more easily reached from the south via Trabuco Canyon and Holy Jim Trail.

On your way back down Modjeska Canyon, turn left around the little road island onto Modjeska Grade, a barber-pole climb that opens briefly onto views of the canyon and the peaks above it then twists around to another view across the tile roofs to the Pacific, and on a clear day, Catalina Island. The road then dips down to rejoin Santiago Canyon Road.

LIVE OAK/TRABUCO

Continue south on Santiago Canyon Road. Our next canyon excursion is up Live Oak Canyon—a left turn heralded by Cook's Corner, a venerable barbecue joint and biker hangout. Cook's Corner is *the* place to eat, rest, see, and be seen in rural, eastern Orange County. You'll most likely see a flotilla of Harley-Davidsons parked out front. Don't be daunted; they're owned by the type of weekend

Cook's Corner on Santiago Canyon Road is popular with weekend warriors and country drivers.

warriors I call Heck's Angels. Cook's Corner is definitely worth a stop.

Live Oak Canyon makes a bend to the south and, four miles along, presents you at the entrance to O'Neill Regional Park, a 270-acre ribbon of parkland with campsites and picnic areas and short hiking trails among oaks and creekside alders and bay laurels. In 1769, Captain Gaspar de Portola's expedition camped on the banks of the stream here as they explored California en route to Monterey. One of Portola's soldiers lost his rifle somewhere in the canyon, which they decided to dub El Trabuco—"the blunderbuss."

If you want to make the trek up Santiago Peak, continue past O'Neill Park, cross the dry wash of Arroyo Trabuco, and turn left up Trabuco Canyon Road. From there it's a 4.7-mile dirt drive past a lot of old cabins and a 15-mile round-trip hike on the Holy Jim Trail, but well worth the effort on a clear day for a panoramic view that's like a topographic map of Southern California come to life.

Now, I hate to do this to you, but remember, this is Orange County. To continue a tour of the Santa Ana Mountains, you'll have to endure an interlude of suburb and freeway. Continue past O'Neill Park, enjoy a few more views of Santiago Peak, then emerge in a massive housing development called Rancho Santa Margarita. Turn down Santa Margarita Parkway to El Toro Road and left on El Toro Road to Interstate 5, the Santa Ana Freeway. Take the freeway south about 10 miles to the Ortega Highway exit in San Juan Capistrano.

ORTEGA HIGHWAY

The Ortega Highway, State Highway 74, is the only through road in the Santa Ana Mountains. In linking San Juan Capistrano and Lake Elsinore, it climbs through rugged, corrugated foothills, skirts the rim of San Juan

San Juan Picnic Area is one of many tranquil spots in the Cleveland National Forest near the Ortega Highway.

Canyon, and peaks out in a mixed oak and conifer forest at 2,666 feet. It's a fast road, but the scenery begs a slower pace. Fortunately, once you enter Cleveland National Forest, turnouts are frequent.

The highway takes its name from Jose Francisco Ortega, a sergeant in the Portola expedition and presumably not the one who left his blunderbuss behind. The route follows a way first blazed by the Juaneno Indians. It was a wagon road at the turn of the century and a proper roadway since 1933.

Begin by turning left (east) from the freeway off-ramp. (The famous San Juan Capistrano Mission is just a half-mile away should you elect to turn right.) You'll soon clear the suburbs, pass a relict orange grove, and come to Caspers Regional Park.

This park in the rugged foothills is the only park I know of that is X-rated: Children under 18 are not allowed. The prohibition dates to the mid-1980s, when two highly publicized mountain lion maulings of children provoked mountain-lion hysteria. The shy creatures whose habitat has been severely crimped the last few decades are very rarely seen, but the park, aware of its potential liability, retains a stricture against kids—and against solo hiking for adults. About 30 miles of trails criss-cross this old ranch property, and a visitor center interprets the natural and native human history of the area.

Ortega Highway continues slicing into the Santa Anas and enters Cleveland National Forest, following the course of San Juan Creek. A picnic area and a campground provide easy access to the shady riffle. The steep, chaparral-covered slopes above are dotted with granite boulders. At the road's first crest, about 20 miles from San Juan Capistrano, are a country store, private campground, and parking for the San Juan Loop Trail, a popular hike that takes in a San Juan Creek waterfall, a welcome sight on a dusty summer day.

SECRET SIDE LOOP

Just before Ortega Highway makes its final crest and drops down to Elsinore, it enters a shady area known as El Cariso. Among the dense oaks are a country store, some scattered dwellings, and a campground. Because the campground is right on the highway, it's rather noisy. For a quieter spot, and the prettiest paved drive in the Santa Anas, take the left turn just beyond El Cariso Campground. This loop road climbs to quiet, secluded Blue Jay Campground. En route, it snakes around a high ridge with successive views of Lake Elsinore, the San Jacinto Mountains, the San Bernardino Mountains, and the southern portion of the Santa Anas. Fluffy buckwheat blossoms line the road, with bright yellow Spanish broom and bush sunflowers providing splashes of color. The return portion of the loop offers an aerial view of the oak tufts that shade El Cariso. It's a narrow, untrammeled road, about a seven-mile loop, that returns you to Highway 74 just below El Cariso.

Beyond El Cariso, Ortega Highway reaches its apex at only 2,666 feet, which accounts for the paucity of conifers. As the road makes a sweeping descent toward Lake

Elsinore, you feel like you're circling for a landing. A couple of turnouts allow you to pause and safely enjoy the view.

LAKE ELSINORE

Perhaps the kindest thing to say about Lake Elsinore is that it's a natural lake. But that means its level is subject to the whims of Southern California's mutable rainfall cycle. Even when full, it rests rather bleakly in a broad basin and has recently seen rampant development around its banks. It's a top-notch bass lake and popular with the waterskiing and jet-skiing crowd, but the state recreation area (campground and marina) on its northern shore is pretty tattered and uninviting.

Palm trees seem to sprout from the middle of the lake when Lake Elsinore is at high water.

Highway 74 follows this shoreline, wends through the town of Elsinore, and meets Interstate 15. From here you can go south a few miles toward Murietta and pick up Tour 11, or head north to your chosen route back to Los Angeles: the Riverside Freeway (91), the Pomona Freeway (60), or Interstate 10.

TOUR 13

Joshua Tree National Park

165 miles
*Cabazon • Big Morongo Canyon Preserve • Joshua Tree •
Hidden Valley • Keys View • Geology Trail • Jumbo Rocks
• Oasis Visitor Center • Twentynine Palms Inn •
Fortynine Palms Canyon • Indian Cove • Pinto Basin •
Cottonwood Visitor Center • Mecca Hills*

Joshua trees: I like to think of them as yuccas with personality. One contingent of botanists contends that they are
lilies of the desert. Captain John C. Frémont called them
"the most repulsive tree in the vegetable kingdom."
Mormon pioneers thought they looked like a hirsute Old
Testament patriarch imploring them onward to the
Promised Land. They called them Joshua trees, and the
name stuck. Like the saguaro of the Sonoran Desert, Joshua
trees, repulsive or not, stand as the symbol of California's
Mojave Desert. In Joshua Tree National Park, the gnarled
yuccas grow in profusion amid rock-pile wonderlands in a
500,000-acre park set aside as the jewel of the Mojave.

This tour encompasses the paved roads of the park,
which lead to most of the scenic attractions. If you're will-

139

ing to stretch your legs a bit, you can get closer to the natural attractions as well as some man-made sites that remain as reminders of the area's quirky human history.

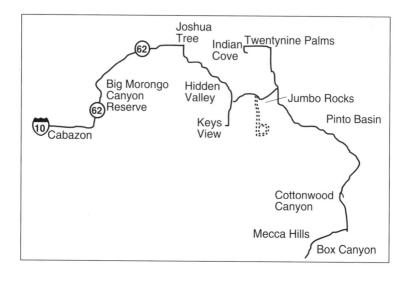

To begin the tour: Take Interstate 10 east from Los Angeles toward Palm Springs, then State Highway 62 to the town of Joshua Tree. Turn right on Park Boulevard, which is the approach to Joshua Tree National Park's west entrance.

DATES WITH DINOSAURS

Before we get to the park, I can't resist pointing out a few highlights en route from Los Angeles. On I-10 in the Banning Pass area are two Southern California landmarks each worth a stop. One is Hadley's, which has been tempting travelers with date shakes since 1931. It's a good place to stock up on munchies for your desert tour, like dried fruits and nuts and, of course, plump dates from the nearby Coachella Valley. Just down the road—you can't miss them—standing guard over the Wheel Inn Cafe are two giant concrete dinosaurs nearly 60 feet high. The structures were the loving creations of Claude Bell, who owned the cafe next door and needed a way to lure travelers in off the freeway. With experience gained from making concrete sculptures at Knott's Berry Farm, Bell framed the dinosaurs in steel and added a concrete epidermis five inches thick. Having withstood the powerful winds of the San Gorgonio Pass for over 20 years, they're not likely to go extinct anytime soon. Inside one of them is a great dinosaur gift shop where you can find all sorts of mementos for the dino lovers in your family.

Soon after you diverge on State Highway 62, you'll pass through the small town of Morongo Valley. Turn right at the well-marked sign for Big Morongo Canyon Preserve, a Nature Conservancy preserve that is one of the Mojave's hidden gems. A high water table and generously flowing

The 60-foot concrete dinosaurs of Cabazon are a landmark to travelers on I-10 headed to Joshua Tree or Palm Springs. A dinosaur gift shop is nestled in the viscera of the one in the foreground.

perennial springs make Big Morongo Canyon a lush oasis and a magnet for birds and other wildlife. It's great fun to take the Mesquite/Canyon trail and savor the anomaly of such lush wetness in the arid desert. The trail begins as a boardwalk over the springs. A thatch of thick mesquite provides cool shade, and the clear water flows over wild watercress. The walk continues into the arid canyon where the water eventually disappears underground.

Highway 62 stairsteps in elevation and stutters through stoplights in the booming desert towns of Yucca Valley (see Tour 15) and Joshua Tree. By the time you reach the park entrance, you've climbed from the low Colorado Desert near Palm Springs to the high Mojave Desert of this part of Joshua Tree. The road through the west entrance quickly gives you a sense of the majesty of the place. You crest a rise and suddenly you're in a realm of huge rocks and fantastically grotesque Joshua trees.

The visitor center for the park is not at this west entrance, but at the north entrance near the town of Twentynine Palms. I prefer to enter from the west to minimize backtracking, but if you wish to pick up literature on the park and see a few natural history exhibits, by all means continue on Highway 62 to Twentynine Palms, about 12 miles. You will, however, receive a park map at the west entrance station.

The usual desert caveats apply to driving and hiking in Joshua Tree. Check with the visitor center on road conditions before venturing off paved roads. Most importantly, carry a lot of water, for there is no water (nor flush toilets) within the monument. Occasionally there's a water tank at some of the campgrounds, but don't count on it. If you're camping, bring at least two gallons per person per day. Otherwise, carry at least one gallon per person per day. Spring and fall are the most pleasant times to visit—spring always brings the possibility of a wildflower show. This being high desert, winter can be cold with occasional snowfall. In the central part of the monument, daytime highs are in the 50s in winter, 70s in spring and fall, and 90s in summer. No need to rule out a summer visit—just plan activities like hiking for the morning or late afternoon. Nights are pleasant and cool.

JOSHUA TREE FOREST

As you proceed toward Hidden Valley, you pass through "forests" of Joshua trees. These might look pretty sparse and tattered to be regarded as forests, but each tree has to spread its roots widely to lap up moisture in the sand; so this is about as thick as a Joshua tree forest gets. Of course, the Joshua tree is not a tree at all. Its botanical name is *Yucca brevifolia*—short-leaf yucca. I'd read for years that the Joshua was a member of the lily family, but lately it seems to be grouped with the agave clan. Lily or not, it does put out clusters of creamy white blossoms, a delicate (though not too fragrant) touch on a plant characterized by gnarled shape, rough bark, and dagger-like leaves.

Grotesque or arabesque, the forms of Joshua trees are as individual and provocative as clouds. Each tree seems to

The essence of Joshua Tree National Park: quiet roads, Joshua trees, rock formations, and lots of open space.

attempt to mock or outdo its nearby brethren as they grow in twisted shapes up to 40 feet high. J. Smeaton Chase, that lover and wanderer of the desert early in this century, observed in *California Desert Trails*, "A landscape filled with Joshua trees has a nightmare effect in broad daylight; at the witching hour it can be almost infernal."

The Joshua is hardly infernal to the wildlife that rely on it. At least 25 bird species nest in its seemingly inhospitable spines. Look across a forest of Joshua trees and you're almost certain to see a hawk perched in one of them. Lizards, packrats, and woodrats rely on the Joshua tree for shelter. One Joshua denizen, the yucca moth, is responsible for the tree's procreation. Indians utilized Joshua tree flower buds and seeds for food, and fibers from the leaves for sandals and nets. Pioneers used the wood for fencing material. Though soft and light, Joshua tree wood is obviously adapted to desert life and, therefore, extremely durable. One failed scheme of the 1880s had Joshua trees supplying pulp for paper mills. And during a Southern California land boom of the 1880s, real estate con men impaled cheap windfall oranges on the ends of Joshua tree spines hoping to entice some naive easterners into signing on the bottom line.

PILES OF ROCK

Complementing the weird shapes of the Joshua trees in Hidden Valley and throughout the monument are massive piles of rocks that often seem to have been delicately balanced atop one another. Who had the time and energy to stack all these rocks? Well, the quartz monzonite that makes up these rocks was once a molten liquid that was forced upward but cooled before reaching the surface. Groundwater seeped downward along joints, creating fractures that divided the rocks. Later, as floods washed away groundcover and exposed the rocks, further erosion

Joshua Tree is the winter arena for rock climbers from all over the world. Here a climber on belay from above completes a pitch in Hidden Valley.

attacked the weakened joints, creating the effect of rock piles and forming boulders into fantastic shapes.

Glance at the rocks when you arrive at the Hidden Valley picnic area and you may see huge reptilian creatures creeping slowly up the rock faces. Look closer. They're humans. Rock climbers, to be exact. In winter and spring, Joshua Tree is *the* spot in the world for rock climbing. The pitches aren't very high compared to, say, El Capitan in Yosemite. But the extremely high friction quality of the rock and the sheer number of routes to climb make Joshua Tree fabled among climbers. Many set up camp for weeks at a time. Entire thick guidebooks are dedicated to identifying and rating some 4,500 climbs in "J-Tree," as the climbers call it.

Climbers generally work in pairs: One climbs while the other holds him on belay. The belay is for protection in case of a fall, not for assistance with the climb. Proud climbers always attempt to "free climb" the rock faces and cracks

without any direct aid. Climbers in J-Tree also enjoy bouldering—working on their strength and moves on smaller
rocks, without belay. If they fall, they simply jump to the
ground, unhurt. Try a little bouldering yourself. You'll
quickly learn how high-friction the monzonite is. Wearing
ordinary sneakers or hiking boots, you can walk up surprisingly steep faces without any assistance, even from
your hands.

HIDDEN VALLEY

A trail through Hidden Valley puts you in close contact
with some of the monument's fabled rock. Huge boulders
and rock piles virtually enclose much of the 1.4-mile loop
trail through a valley that, in a time of greater rainfall, once
grew tall grass. Signs along the trail tell the story of the
McHaney brothers, cattlemen who were pretty successful
here for a time, thanks either to the grass or their deft abili-
ty at altering the brands on neighboring ranchers' cattle.

Across the way, out of Hidden Valley Campground,
another short trail leads to an improbable site called Barker
Dam, a concrete catchment that forms a good-size pond in
wet years. It also leads to some of the most vivid petroglyphs in the entire Mojave Desert. Unfortunately, these
were painted by a Hollywood film crew to add a touch of
"realism" to this site during the filming of a western.

Also near here are the well-preserved buildings of Desert
Queen Ranch, which can only be visited on a ranger-con-
ducted tour. The ranch was the work of an energetic, dedicated man named Bill Keys (1879–1969) whose knack for
adapting to a harsh environment was most impressive. He
built dams and cisterns to catch water, laid pipes to irrigate
gardens and an orchard, and raised a family on the ranch.
He also ran cattle and worked gold mines. He is buried on
his ranch, which stands as a memorial to the most intrepid
of desert rats.

KEYS VIEW

It's thanks to Bill Keys that we have Keys View Road, a good paved road that leads six miles from the junction with the main park road to a spectacular view at its terminus. Keys built the road in 1926 as access to Hidden Gold Mine, which lies—hidden, of course—2,000 feet below the mile-high viewpoint. Keys View is the crest of a range called the Little San Bernardino Mountains, which drops off abruptly here. The view reveals a distinct transition between the Mojave and Colorado deserts, as these mountains slope steeply down to the sparsely vegetated low-desert floor, which extends to the base of the San Jacinto Mountains. In between are the shimmering sea-level towns of the Coachella Valley. To the south, you might see as far as the below-sea-level Salton Sea.

JUMBO GEOLOGY

After you make the out-and-back jaunt to Keys View, return to the park road and turn right. The road passes through Sheep Pass—at 4,000 feet, prime Joshua tree territory. Some of the largest Joshuas in the Mojave are between Sheep's Pass and Jumbo Rocks.

Beyond Sheep's Pass you can take an educational field trip on the 18-mile Geology Tour Road. The road is dirt, but most of it is smooth and well graded. An informative pamphlet, keyed to numbered stops along the way, is available at the head of the road. By the time you return, you'll be an expert on alluvial fans and pinto gneiss (the dark stuff of the mountain ranges within the monument). Plus, with a little footwork, you can see petroglyphs and old mines.

Back again on the park road, you'll soon come to the Jumbo Rocks area, where there's a campground, picnic area, and, you guessed it . . . rocks. Big ones. These rocks are favorites of those who like to anthropomorphize. Take the

Skull Rock Trail to a rounded chunk of monzonite with skull-like concavities.

OASIS OF MARA

From Jumbo Rocks, the road bends north toward the north entrance to the park and the town of Twentynine Palms. Park headquarters and the Oasis Visitor Center are on your left shortly after you exit the park. The visitor center has a good bookstore, and among the exhibits are pictures of Bill Keys and his family during the heyday of Desert Queen Ranch. Be sure to check the calendar for guided ranger walks, evening programs (held in outdoor amphitheaters in Jumbo Rocks and Indian Cove campgrounds), and tours of Desert Queen Ranch (usually on Saturday). One guided hike focuses on desert survival techniques and visits the grave of Matt Riley, "someone who should have attended this program."

The visitor center borders on the fan-palm Oasis of Mara, and a short nature trail passes through it. No water is visible on the surface (nearby wells have pumped it away), but the palms and mesquite trees flourish, thanks to a shallow water table. The oasis has been a home, watering hole, and resting site for Indians for many years and for early white

Coyotes are usually nocturnal and wary, but this wily fellow has probably received handouts from campers and has lost some of his healthy fear of man.

pioneers. They called it Mara—"land of little rain." (Twentynine Palms gets about four inches per year.) An 1855 survey of the area recorded 26 palm trees around the oasis, which was called Palm Springs. But then someone must have counted three more trees, and the new name stuck. The community of Twentynine Palms grew after World War I when a Pasadena doctor sent some of his disabled-veteran patients out to the desert for a cure. It worked, and many health-seekers remained.

TWENTYNINE PALMS INN

Bordering the Oasis of Mara on the opposite side from the visitor center is a wonderful hostelry that has been hosting desert visitors since 1928. It's still in the same family. Don't expect the uniform, synthesized, predictable ways of a chain hotel at the Twentynine Palms Inn. Nothing is normal here, but everything is charming. As the entrance sign proclaims, "we discourage misery and offer alternatives."

Guest rooms are nine adobe bungalows scattered about the oasis and roughly framing a shady lagoon. Another room is a frame bungalow transplanted from an old mining settlement called Gold Park. In layout and decor, the rooms can only be described as quirky. The rooms have no phones, and you can't buy a newspaper. Killer geese honk around the grounds demanding, "Your bread crumbs or your life." The poolside restaurant/bar (the food is excellent) is also the office. What seems to be the office is more like a library, and sells lamps cleverly made from yucca stalks. It's all perfectly appropriate for the Mojave Desert, which is no one's notion of a symmetrical paradise, like, say, the Swiss Alps. But the place has lately caught the attention of avant-garde art directors—several fashion magazines have staged shoots at the inn. To get there, turn left on Monument Drive from Utah Street, the street that fronts the visitor center.

FORTYNINE PALMS AND MORE

Both Monument Road and Utah Street lead to Highway 62, which is the main drag for the town of Twentynine Palms. The town today is mainly known for a nearby Marine Corps base, so it naturally has a lot of barbershops plus convenience stores to serve desert tourists. Turn left on Highway 62 to visit two of the monument's northern attractions. One is Fortynine Palms Oasis, a remote canyon oasis that's a worthy reward for a rocky, two-mile hike. Canyon Road, just west of town, leads to the trailhead.

A bit farther west is the well-marked sign for Indian Cove. This site has camping and picnicking, but I go here for the rocks. You *think* you've seen rocks—sure, J-Tree is full of rocks—but not like Wonderland of Rocks at Indian Cove. Wonderland of Rocks is like a universe compared to a galaxy—a long chain of rock piles with wondrous forms and great climbs. You can walk up a wash through Rattlesnake Canyon and be surrounded by the wonderland. If you begin to sense that there's life in the rock, you're getting the hang of the desert.

HIGH DESERT, LOW DESERT

Until now, we've been roaming the central and northern realms of J-Tree—all high desert. It's easy to tell high from low if by no other indicator than Joshua trees which prefer life around 3,000 to 4,000 feet. But Joshua Tree National Park also contains a large swath of low desert and a distinctive transition zone in between.

First, retrace your route past the visitor center and return to the park through the north entrance. Stay to the left at the intersection (a right would take you back to Jumbo Rocks) and pass Belle and White Tank campgrounds. As this road descends toward the Cottonwood Visitor Center, you'll probably notice some changes: fewer pink-tinged archipel-

A beavertail cactus in bloom is one of the colorful sights of Joshua Tree in the spring.

agos of quartz monzonite, fewer Joshua trees, then no Joshua trees. Plants might be in bloom that haven't yet opened in the higher elevations—creosote and brittlebush might be blossoming in yellow. Spreading out below you is the vast Pinto Basin, dappled in dark hues by creosote bushes and the iron-manganese "desert varnish" of the basin floor.

As you come around one bend in the road, you suddenly see a vast spread of fuzz-fringed cholla cactus eponymously called the Cholla Garden. Cholla is a "gotcha" cactus that has the annoying habit of shedding its prickly joints. So while you're carefully walking so as not to brush the spiny plant, one of the little broken-off spine-balls has found its way to your shoe or sock. They can be hard to remove—a pocket comb works best. The cholla's tendency to get you despite precautions has earned it the name "jumping cholla." And for its fuzzy guise (not to be trusted), it is sometimes called "teddy bear cholla."

Just down the road from Cholla Garden is Ocotillo Patch. The tall, spindly ocotillo is, like the cholla, an indicator plant for the Colorado Desert. The long, gangly limbs sprout green leaves after rainfall and red-orange blossoms in spring.

The park road then descends into the heart of Pinto Basin, vast, spacious, almost foreboding in its austerity. Clumps of creosote are the only signs of life. I suggest stopping for a walk in Pinto Basin, if only for a hundred yards or to a clump of rocks, to fully feel that heavy-atmosphere sense of being surrounded by so much open space.

At Cottonwood, there's a scaled-down version of a visitor center, a campground, and a trail to a man-made oasis called Cottonwood Spring. The water is natural, but the palms and cottonwoods were planted early in the century.

South of the Cottonwood Visitor Center, the road keeps descending. After Cottonwood Pass, it crosses a classic low-desert wash, full of smoke trees and palo verde, before reaching Interstate 10. To return to Los Angeles, take Interstate 10 west, and on the way back, stop at the General Patton Memorial Museum. The museum commemorates General George Patton's desert maneuvers of 1942—training for the North African campaign that was crucial to the Allied victory in World War II. Patton explained his strategy to his officers: "If you can work successfully here, in this country, it will be no difficulty at all to kill the assorted sons of bitches you meet in any other country."

If you prefer a dramatic alternative to the inevitable freeway return, cross over the interstate, turn right, and take Box Canyon Road to Mecca. This lonely stretch of road drops from Pinto Basin into a dramatic cleft of the Mecca Hills. It slides for miles between sedimentary cliffs until it emerges into the different, that is, irrigated, world, of the Salton Sea's north shore. From here you can take State Highway 195 to Highway 86 and join Tour 17 around the Salton Sea; or take Highway 111 toward Palm Springs and join Tour 8; or take Highway 111 to Interstate 10 west to Los Angeles.

TOUR 14

The East Mojave

175 miles
*Baker • Kelso Depot • Kelso Dunes • Nipton • Ivanpah •
Caruthers Canyon • Mid Hills • Hole-in-the-Wall •
Mitchell Caverns*

To anyone familiar with Southern California, the coordinates "east of Barstow and west of Needles" describe, quite simply the Middle of Nowhere. The Mojave National Preserve (formerly East Mojave National Scenic Area) is a swath of high desert and mountains that has received some political notoriety in recent years, but remains a vast and lonely place. Many more people express opinions about the East Mojave than visit it, which is to our benefit; for despite the hubbub, the scenic area retains most of the character that makes the desert such a compelling place to visit. "Character" can be enumerated as canyons, buttes, dunes, mines, mountains, washes, basins, lava flows, and cinder cones, or wildlife—coyotes, bighorn sheep, chuckwalla lizards, and desert tortoises. But the allure of the East Mojave has more to do with space: an unbroken largeness of sky and land that renders everything else mere details. Interesting details, sure, but it is 1.5 million acres of spaciousness that stirs the spirit here. In the East Mojave you can gain a high vantage and see nothing man-made for 60 miles except the road that got you there.

The East Mojave was the nexus of a hotly debated conservation plan for the California desert for over a decade.
At the end of 1994, President Clinton signed a bill that created what conservationists had long sought: Mojave
National Preserve. For years it had been under the multi-
ple-use management of the Bureau of Land Management,
which allowed grazing and mining within the borders of
the scenic area. Those activities will continue in the national preserve, but eventually will be phased out. Large tracts
have been set aside as wilderness, which has drawn the ire
of off-road vehicle enthusiasts even though most current
Jeep trails will remain open.

Personally, my fear is that the National Park Service will
bring national park niceties to the East Mojave. As it is, the
East Mojave is not a particularly easy place to visit, and
therein lies part of its mystique. A lot of the roads are
unpaved, the toilets don't flush, and you pump water by
hand. Will the national preserve bring a network of fast
paved roads, a designer visitor center, sign pollution, and
thousands more visitors every year? I don't know. I'll be
happy to encounter fewer cow flops, fences, and buzz-saw
dirt bikes when I hike through the backcountry, but unhap-
py to find Yosemite-style cafeterias and gas stations. My
fears may be unfounded. Maybe the National Park Service
will be able to resist its compulsion to impose contrived convenience on wild places. But my advice stands: See it now.

To begin the tour: The East Mojave lies between Interstates
15 and 40 about 60 miles east of Barstow. The tour I recommend enters the national preserve from the north.
From Los Angeles, take Interstate 10 to I-15 north toward
Barstow. It's a good idea to stop in Barstow at the
California Desert Information Center to pick up maps and
information on weather and road conditions. The Center
is at 831 Barstow Road—take the Central Barstow exit

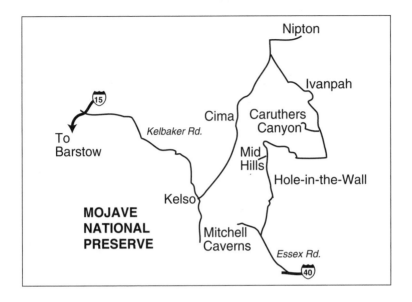

from I-15 and proceed one block north. Then continue on I-15 about 60 miles to the Kelbaker Road exit. Turn right (south) on Kelbaker Road.

KELBAKER ROAD

As soon as you start south on Kelbaker Road, you see a sign that holds great promise for the experience ahead: "Next services 76 miles." (If you don't have a full tank of gas and plenty of water and food, make a U-turn and stock up in the town of Baker.) The immediate reward is an escape from the Las Vegas circus train. And then, slowly, what seems from the interstate like a vast void comes into focus. You first notice a lot of black rock. No fewer than 30 cinder cones dot this volcanic area, and the black basalt they spewed forms a 400-foot-thick overlay atop a base of granite. Apollo astronauts trained in this area before the first moon landing. Enjoy the sight from your car, or turn up Aiken's Mine Road, a good dirt road, to explore the lava beds first hand.

As Kelbaker Road climbs, you enter a zone of Joshua trees, which favor elevations in the 3,000- to 4,000-foot range. Atop a rise, you get your first look at the Providence Mountains, an impressive, jagged massif rising over 7,000 feet. The sight typifies the East Mojave, a land of basin and range. That anomalous straight line you see is the Union Pacific Railroad, and standing next to it in an area of obvious oasis is the even more startling sight of a whitewashed, Spanish-tile-roofed structure. This once-elegant building is/was Kelso Depot. The little town of Kelso arose when the Los Angeles to Salt Lake City rail line was completed in 1906. Water found just underground at this oasis once supplied the steam locomotives that plied the line. Union Pacific built the depot in 1924 and abandoned it in 1985. Efforts are underway to restore it, perhaps as a visitor center for the national preserve.

Kelso Depot, built in 1924 to serve the Union Pacific Railroad, stands near Kelbaker Road. It may one day serve as a visitor center for Mojave National Preserve.

Booming Dunes

Dunes that boom? Not only do Kelso Dunes have musical talent, they're one of the landmark sights of the East Mojave, wonderfully sculpted like cake frosting and peaking as high as 700 feet. To get to the dunes, cross the railroad tracks at Kelso and continue south another eight miles to a signed dirt road that leads three miles to the dunes. The road may be washboard, but it's always passable. It's about a 10-minute walk from the parking area to the dunes. When you get close and into the dunes, you find that the sand mountains are dotted with slender grasses and tender wild-

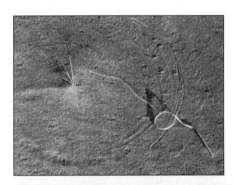

Inscription of dune grass denotes shifting breezes in Kelso Dunes.

Rugged Providence Mountains loom as a backdrop to Kelso Dunes.

flowers—verbena, primrose, and desert sunflowers. You'll also come across some willows.

The booming? It doesn't happen every day, but quite often, as sand avalanches or blowing sands pass over the underlying layer, they emit a low rumble that sounds something like a kettle drum.

NIPTON

Backtrack now to Kelso and turn right on Kelso-Cima Road. If you need a snack, stop in at the Cima Store, which is the town of Cima in its entirety and the only commercial facility within the national preserve. If you want to see one of the densest Joshua tree forests in the desert, turn left on Cima Road to the Cima Dome area, just a few miles north. The thing about Cima Dome, a 75-mile dome of nearly pure symmetry, is that you can't tell you're on a dome while you're on it. It shows up best on a topographical map or from the air.

The four-room Hotel Nipton is an oasis bed-and-breakfast retreat amid vast desert solitude.

To continue the tour, proceed north on Morning Star Mine Road and turn left on Ivanpah Road then right on Nipton Road to the time-warp "town" of Nipton, once a mining town and a station on the Union Pacific line. Nipton consists mainly of a well-stocked country store that seems to specialize above all in selling lottery tickets, and the one-of-a-kind Nipton Hotel. The bed-and-breakfast hotel has four tiny but charming rooms, with facilities down the hall, but the price is right and there's an outdoor hot tub and a great nighttime star show. Inside, an old black and white photo shows the hotel and cactus garden circa 1930. Nothing appears to have changed in the ensuing years. It's nice to say that about *some* place. There's even a sign in one of the rooms that informs you, "This room is equipped with Edison electric light. Do not attempt to light. Simply turn key by door."

PLAYING IN THE DIRT

Ready for some serious exploration? Much of the remaining portion of the tour is on dirt roads. These roads are wide and well graded, but unless they've been recently regraded, they can turn to washboard in stretches. Just go slowly. You can easily get by with two-wheel drive.

From Nipton, return to Ivanpah Road and go south. Ivanpah soon turns to dirt and passes by the site of an 1890s gold-mining town called Vanderbilt. Cornelius had nothing to do with the place. The miners simply co-opted his name for good luck. They had some—a town of 3,000 once flourished here. A few ruins of buildings remain.

Ivanpah Road slithers through a pass in the New York Mountains. One wonders if national preserve status will eliminate such sights along the way as the upended carcass of a 1958 Studebaker that has probably been decaying ever-so-slowly here (things don't rust fast in these parts) since, well, 1958. The road soon settles into the Ivanpah Valley, the stomping grounds, so to speak, for the desert tortoise. If one

*Extraordinary solitude reigns
in the East Mojave, even along
such main routes as Ivanpah
Road. Such roads are easily
passable by two-wheel drive.*

darts across your path, resist the temptation to handle it.
Let him scuttle on in peace—the tortoise is a threatened
species and can do without the trauma of human intrusion
into his busy life. A bumpy side trip into the mountains on
New York Mountains Road is highly worthwhile. The road
leads to Caruthers Canyon, my favorite camping place in
the East Mojave (although there's no water), and an odd
biological island. Caruthers harbors a community of chaparral plants that belong in the coastal mountains: oaks,
manzanita, and ceanothus. It also has some shady stands of
pinyon pines and juniper.

As Ivanpah Road continues southward, it enters Lanfair
Valley. The intersection of Ivanpah (which south of here is
called Lanfair Road) and Cedar Canyon was once the site of
a town called Lanfair populated by ranchers and homesteaders. Unusually wet weather early in the century lured
a number of would-be farmers to the area. They hoped to
emulate the success of Edwin Lanfair, who came in 1910

This old Studebaker has settled into the landscape of the East Mojave.

and raised wheat and barley in the valley. But cattle ranchers were hostile to the farmers and refused them access to water, so after years of hostility and violence, the homesteaders gave up. A few ranches remain in the valley today.

MID HILLS AND HOLE-IN-THE-WALL

Turn right on Cedar Canyon Road. You're now paralleling the course of the Mojave Road and at times coinciding with the historical trail. The Mojave Road was blazed by Indians traveling from the Colorado River to the coast. It connected vital watering holes that made the journey possible. Later, 1820s explorers such as Jedediah Smith and Kit Carson followed the route, which eventually stretched from Prescott, Arizona, to Los Angeles. By the 1860s it became a frontier freeway, which didn't please the local Indians. To protect the carriers for the Arizona Overland Mail and other travelers, the Army established Fort Piute, the ruins of which are east of Ivanpah Road and, like much of the Mojave Trail, accessible only by four-wheel drive.

At the intersection with Black Canyon Road, turn south toward Hole-in-the-Wall Campground. After a short distance, you can turn west and make a two-mile detour to Mid Hills Campground, the most popular camping spot in the East Mojave. And for good reason. There's water and lots of shade amid thick stands of pinyon pine and juniper. (When Euell Gibbons used to tell us that parts of a pine tree were edible, he probably had pine nuts, the creamy white product of the pinyon, in mind.) At 5,600 feet, Mid Hills is often cooler than lower parts of the national preserve. It's also a good vantage point for identifying some of the East Mojave's landforms: You can even make out Cima Dome to the northwest.

Continue down toward Hole-in-the-Wall. You'll be driving in the shadow of the Providence Mountains on your right. Over to the east is Table Top, a circular, flat-topped mountain (6,176 feet) that looks like a backdrop in a Charles Russell painting. The scrub range on either side of the road is grazing land, some of it private and some of it leased from the federal government.

Even if you're not camping, Hole-in-the-Wall is a highlight of the East Mojave you shouldn't miss. It's also the headquarters, such as they are, for the national preserve. In other words, there's a little ranger station across the road from the campground.

You might logically think that Hole-in-the-Wall takes its name from the Swiss-cheese concavities in the volcanic formations that form the backdrop to the camping area. But poke around a bit and you'll find the *hole in the wall*, an opening in the rock that leads into Banshee Canyon. To get to that enclosed canyon you have to lower yourself through the hole and down about 25 feet. Steel rings have been placed in the rock to facilitate the maneuver. It's great fun to poke around the rhyolite formations that frame Banshee Canyon or to proceed through it and drop down into Wild Horse Canyon. A Jeep trail in Wild Horse leads up to Mid Hills and a hiking trail parallels it—be sure to take plenty of water if you set out on foot.

MITCHELL CAVERNS

Continue south on Black Canyon Road to the intersection with paved Essex road. Turn right toward Mitchell Caverns Natural Preserve and Providence Mountains State Recreation Area, an island of state park within the national preserve. From the Mitchell Caverns headquarters you have access to hikes among the rhyolite crags of the Providence Mountains. Or you can take a pleasant little self-guiding nature trail. But most folks come up here to see Mitchell Caverns. The rococo chambers are filled with limestone formations—stalagmites, stalactites, flowstone, and an unusual formation called cave shield. Rangers lead tours through two of the caverns. Experienced spelunkers can obtain a permit to explore a third—Winding Stair Cave, which descends 320 feet in a series of sheer drop-offs that vary from 50 to 100 feet. Outside the caverns, you might spot a chuckwalla lizard, a plump, Godzilla-like creature that the Indians considered a delicacy to eat. Chuckwallas will slip into rock cracks and puff up their stomachs to avoid extraction and barbecuing.

A vast and wonderful view unfolds from the headquarters at Mitchell Caverns. If the light is fading or rising, the flatlands look empty, and the punctuating mountain ranges are lavender. In late spring or summer you might see scattered thunderstorms and rainbows. Mostly what you see is space. The vast basin below is about the same size as the Los Angeles basin. But when I survey this one with binoculars, all I see is one lonely ranch house about 10 miles east and a few vultures looking for food.

From Providence Mountains State Recreation Area, go south on Essex Road to Interstate 10 west and back to Los Angeles. Or continue across the interstate to Essex and pick up the National Trails Highway—Old Route 66, described in Tour 18.

Yucca Valley to Barstow: Highway 247

95 miles
Yucca Valley • Pioneertown • Landers • The Integratron •
Lucerne Valley • Barstow • Rainbow Basin • Calico Early
Man Site

Desert visitors often wonder if the desert breeds eccentricity or simply attracts people thus predisposed. Of course, this may all have to do with city folks' snooty ideas about what is normal in the first place.

I don't dwell on the psychology, but I do enjoy the eccentricity of the desert, and I'm thankful that it survives in this era that values emulation, predictability, and synthetic experiences.

This tour doesn't visit any world-renowned beauty spots, nor has anyone proposed making any of it a national park. It's a slice of San Bernardino County, largest county in the Lower 48, by way of an old-fashioned desert highway surrounded by so much open space it can make you feel like a 19th century pioneer. But I enjoy this drive as much for the oddities it links as for any aesthetic notions. Where else can you sleep on a throne-like bed of a Persian suite, visit an Old West movie set, a dome built by aliens, a silver mine, and the archeological home of the earliest Americans, all in a single day or weekend?

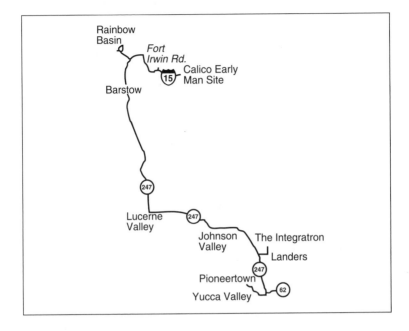

To begin the tour: Take Interstate 10 east from Los Angeles to Highway 62. Follow 62 northeast as it stairsteps from the low Colorado Desert to the high Mojave Desert town of Yucca Valley.

YUCCA VALLEY

By the time you get to Yucca Valley, you're in the high-desert realm of the Joshua tree at 3,327 feet. Since the next town east had already taken the Joshua tree for its name and the Joshua is in the yucca family anyway, Yucca Valley seemed as good a name as any for the town. To its credit, even though Yucca Valley has burgeoned and spawned an infestation of shopping centers and fast-food joints, it has allowed the Joshua trees to remain and flourish.

PIONEERTOWN

Although it has many familiar franchise names, Yucca Valley is not a standard-issue California suburb. For example: As you come into town, watch for the "Pioneertown" sign. Nothing explains what that means, but follow Pioneertown Road about four miles into the rocky hills, and you'll find out. You'll first spot some horse corrals, then the Pioneer Palace—a country-western bar, restaurant, and pool hall. Behind the Pioneer Palace is a wide, dusty street lined sporadically with weathered wood buildings, looking for all the world like a 1940s movie western town, which is exactly what it was.

The town was built on a ranch belonging to Lucky Hayden (a Hopalong Cassidy sidekick) as a reproduction of 19th century Langtry, Texas. Roy Rogers and Gene Autry were among the principals behind the town, and in its heyday, it was common to see the likes of Tex Ritter, Hopalong Cassidy, Leo Carrillo and the Sons of the Pioneers filming or hanging around town.

The wide road behind the Pioneer Palace is called Mane Street (get it?). The frontier-style buildings that line it are now mostly private residences, plus there's a small post office and church. The huge Hay, Grain & Feed building was a sound stage built for the Cisco Kid pictures. Toward the end of Mane Street is Running Deer Park, a kind of Old West village and zoo. A lazy old buffalo and some retired movie deer languish here. If you'd like to share some close quarters with the critters, there's a bunkhouse for rent by the night or week. Return to Yucca Valley the way you came.

DESERT CHRIST

Back on Highway 62, known here as Twentynine Palms Highway, continue east through town and turn left on Mohawk Trail, follow it all the way up hill, and you'll come

Condos are encroaching and some of the statues are shedding limbs, but Antone Martin's Desert Christ Park in Yucca Valley still stands as one of the unique sights of the Mojave Desert.

upon some whitewashed apparitions standing in the sand, sort of a desert Easter Island. The larger-than-life statues were the work of sculptor Antone Martin, who gave the final years of his life (he died in 1961) to building concrete statues depicting scenes from the life of Christ. Thirty-some statues are scattered around the hillside park among shade trees and picnic tables, and there's a huge bas-relief of the Last Supper, 30 feet high. Civilization has crowded up to the base of the park, so the religious figures seem to be gazing down on condominiums and mobile homes; several of the figures suffer from sheared limbs and peeling whitewash. Still, it's a unique place.

OASIS OF EDEN

Lurking among a string of indistinguishable motels along Twentynine Palms Highway is another unique place known as the Oasis of Eden—not your everyday roadside motel. Most of the rooms at the Oasis are theme rooms: the sultan-size bed in the Persian Suite is like a throne in a raised-ceiling chamber; the Ancient Roman Suite has bed-side porticoes and Bacchanalian prints on the walls; the Safari Suite has a canopied bamboo bed and gazelle-themed wallpaper; in the New York, New York Suite you look out from your bed onto the Manhattan skyline and dip into a spa that's almost as big as the bed. And when you sit beside the pool, you see a Baja California beach mural covering the entire length of the poolside wall. The rooms aren't expensive, so the Oasis makes a paradisiacal prologue to an exploration of the area.

Yucca Valley also has one of those great, rambling used book stores called Raven's and a big weekend swap meet at the old Sky Drive-In Theater.

LANDERS: GRUBSTAKE AND THE INTEGRATRON

Head north out of Yucca Valley on State Highway 247, also known as Old Woman Springs Road. After a few miles you'll be on the edge of Landers, which lies mostly to the east between the highway and a lonely butte called Goat Mountain. Few Southern Californians had ever heard of Landers until it was the epicenter of a 7.1 earthquake in 1992. The quake was considerably stronger than the 6.7 Northridge quake in 1994; but lacking much in the way of freeway overpasses or multistory apartment buildings, sparsely populated Landers pulled through reasonably well.

Hungry? Try the Grubstake Inn—desert road food at its finest. Menus are varnished onto wood planks and feature delicacies like chicken-fried steak, fried catfish, and liver and onions. Tasty kitsch festoons the walls and tables, more is on sale at the counter, and if you're lacking for an aphorism, wise sayings are posted on most available wall space.

But you ain't seen nothin' yet. Continue on Highway 247. After a giant dip in the road (they don't make 'em like that anymore), turn right on Reche Road, follow it two miles to Belfield Road, and go about a mile to the end of the pavement.

You can't miss the Integratron. It's the only brilliant white, 40-foot-high, 50-foot-diameter dome in this part of the desert. Although it looks like a concrete space station, its builder, George Van Tassel, made it entirely of wood without using a single nail. It took him 18 years. The exterior is impressive, but the interior really shows Van Tassel's craftsmanship, like that of a fine shipbuilder.

But what is it? "A natural cone of receptivity" is the simple, if vague, answer. Van Tassel was a test pilot for Howard Hughes and counted himself among the privileged fraternity of humans who had contact with alien beings. He was directed to this site by aliens, and like other "power centers" of the world (e.g., the pyramids of Egypt), the Integratron supposedly stands at the intersection of ley lines—invisible meridians of energy in the earth.

But what is it? Stay with me. Through meditation and his alien friends, Van Tassel learned a lot about rejuvenation of the body through electromagnetics. His intent was to build a giant high-voltage electrostatic generator "that would supply a broad range of frequencies to recharge the cell structure." He made it dome-shaped to focus the energies created by a device called a multiple-wave oscillator.

The Integratron in Landers was designed by George Van Tassel, who built the 40-foot wood dome without nails— purportedly at the behest by alien beings.

But what *is* it? Well, Van Tassel died before he was able to complete the project. He planned to use the dome to put into practice the principles of cell rejuvenation by way of a wide range of electromagnetic oscillations. Today the Integratron is a retreat center used by healing and meditation groups. It's open for tours the third and fourth weekend of every month, from noon to 4 p.m. The tour guide will demonstrate the ley line phenomenon with a demonstration of dowsing. Two dowsing rods held lightly in the fists seem to swing out like an open door as you approach the center of the room, then close again. The rods behaved for me exactly as they did for the guide. The guide will also demonstrate a small multiwave oscillator, which bombards you with invisible waves, aligning your cells in the process.

Van Tassel made his home in a cave at nearby Giant Rock, supposedly the largest free-standing boulder in the world and the site of a lot of conventions of UFO contactees. The maze of dirt roads that lead to the boulder can be complicated, and some of them require four-wheel drive. If you don't have four-wheel drive, ask the Integratron tour guide to show you the best way.

MOBY'S DOCK

Return to Highway 247 and continue northwest. Just after Landers Community Church you'll see a "Moby's Dock" sign and a motley squadron of tall, oddly shaped figurines out front. Stan Trempe, who calls himself Moby Dick (he's serious), is the genius behind the carvings. Moby is "retired and retarded," as he says, but a woodcarving savant. The figurines are carved from dead Joshua trees and other oddments of desert wood, and Moby Dick finds the whimsy inherent in each. Some are dinosaurs, some look like giant Gumbies. Trempe is not stuck in a single medium. At Moby's Bar, stools and tables are made from old motorcycle wheels and frames. Most of his creations are for sale,

The "ding-a-lings and things" at Moby's Dock are whimsical statues made from dead Joshua trees, yuccas, and scrapped motorcycles.

Artist Moby Dick shows one of his eccentric wood carvings at his roadside gallery beside Highway 247 near Landers.

as are the fine little dolls his wife, Bobbi, makes. Where does he get ideas for his imaginative figures? "I have lots of bad dreams," Moby Dick answers.

JOHNSON VALLEY HOMESTEADS

As you proceed through Johnson Valley, you'll see dotted about the landscape a number of little shacks approximately the size of Monopoly houses. The shacks indicate an undeveloped homestead, a concept that originated with the Homestead Act of 1862 and the subsequent Desert Lands Act. The idea was to parcel out "farms," each a half-mile square called a quarter-section. The bureaucratic thinking that concocted the scheme assumed east-of-the-Mississippi rainfall. Out here, unless you were lucky enough to have a spring or stream on your quarter-section, you needed a good 2,500 acres to graze livestock, and raising crops was out of the question. The act was a miserable failure, for the most part, and invited all sorts of fraud. For example, each quarter-section was required to have "an erected domicile." If it wasn't a birdhouse, it was a shack. Parcels and "domiciles" are still traded on the desert real estate market. And, once in a while, someone erects a real domicile and they eke out a life in the desert.

Eking is a way of life out here. Signs along the road indicate how some desert people earn a living: "Blacksmith— Custom Art in Steel"; "Peacocks for Sale"; "Oasis Bird Ranch"; "For Sale: Bird Baths, Ocotillo"; "Hay, Scratch, Feed."

As you drive this wide-open stretch of road, the San Bernardino Mountains rise high above you to the west, scarred with mines and mining roads. To the east, some of the open land is the Johnson Valley OHV Area, BLM land given over to off-highway vehicle recreation. The low ranges and mountains farther east belong to the Twentynine Palms Marine Corps Base, and they're used for air-ground combat exercises.

LUCERNE VALLEY

Forty-four miles from Yucca Valley, you come to the little crossroads town of Lucerne Valley, which must have more second-hand stores per capita than any town in the world. Lucerne Valley bears little resemblance to the Swiss town and lake of the same name, although it too is ringed with mountains and it does claim a lake. Lucerne's, though, is a bone-dry affair just north of town.

State Highway 18 leads south out of Lucerne to the San Bernardino Mountains and Big Bear Lake, or west to Apple Valley. But our tour turns north here, staying with State Highway 247.

This is a classic old desert drive, linking the old mining town, Lucerne Valley, with the old transportation center, Barstow. Few signs of habitation intrude upon your views as you pass through creosote flats, then climb a low pass between the Ord Mountains to the east and Stoddard Ridge to the west.

BARSTOW

Highway 247 leads you into Barstow and becomes Barstow Road. You'll cross Interstate 15 and pass by the Desert Information Center operated by the Bureau of Land Management—a good place to pick up maps and books on the California desert.

Barstow was a dusty mining town that grew considerably when the Santa Fe Railroad was completed through Cajon Pass in 1885. It was originally called Grape Vine Station, then renamed in 1886 to honor William Barstow Strong, president of the Santa Fe Railroad.

When you turn left on Main Street in Barstow, you pass through a little bit of Downtown USA, with vintage motels and coffee shops showing a little more character than those that line the freeway corridor. Today, Barstow's claims to fame are primarily factory-outlet shopping and the world's busiest McDonald's, which serves the perpetual Los Angeles-Las Vegas interstate caravan.

RAINBOW BASIN

From Main Street, turn right, cross the railroad tracks and follow the signs for State Highway 58 and Fort Irwin. Don't turn on Highway 58, but continue instead toward Fort Irwin until you reach the turnoff (Fossil Bed Road) for Rainbow Basin National Natural Landmark. Pictorial signs warn of tortoises crossing, and, in fact, along this good dirt road is the only place I've seen a desert tortoise in recent years. It leads three miles to the entrance to Rainbow Basin.

Rainbow Basin is a geology wonder-drive through a multihued canyon of sedimentary layers. About two million years ago, this area was dotted with lakes, and all manner of exotic animals lived along the shores—rhinos, mastodons, camels, the works—and many are fossilized in the sediments that make up the canyon walls. The road slides right through the heart of the canyon. In places,

Desert tortoises are a threatened species in the high Mojave Desert, so motorists en route to Rainbow Basin are urged to be cautious should one attempt to dart across the road.

Rainbow Basin looks like it was made yesterday as a child's mud-sculpting project. In others, the smooth contours are tilted and faulted, obvious signs of earthquake action. Don't wait for a trail or interpretive sign to get you out of the car. There aren't any. But do pull over at a wide spot in the one-way loop road and explore a wash or side canyon. On weekdays, you'll have little company, and Rainbow Basin feels like a holy, ancient place.

CALICO GHOST TOWN

A re-creation of an 1890s gold-mining town developed by Walter Knott of Knott's Berry Farm fame may sound like a recipe for a tourist trap, but Calico has authentic roots as a silver-mining boom town, and the re-creation is well done. Sure, it has tacky gift shops, shooting galleries, and the like. But it also has a tour through one of the original silver mines, the Maggie, a train ride, and excellent examples of the crude dugout caves many miners called home.

To get there, retrace your way back to the paved Fort Irwin Road. Follow it briefly toward Fort Irwin, then turn right (south) toward Barstow. Then take the Yermo cutoff to the left, which leads to Ghost Town Road and Calico. Huge white letters on the side of the rusty red mountain spell it out for you: "CALICO."

Calico produced over $86 million in silver ore between first strike in 1881 and a fall in the price of silver in 1896. In its heyday, it handily supported 22 saloons and a population of 4,000. Walter Knott purchased it in 1951, restored it, then turned it over to the county, which runs it as a historical park. Tourist trap, maybe, but Calico is fun.

EARLIEST MAN

Most experts agreed for a long time that no humans were in North America until about 12,000 years ago. So imagine the experts' surprise when stone tools were found near a cat-litter mine outside Barstow, scientifically dated to be 200,000 years old, give or take 20,000 years. The big question was, and is: Were these really tools or just odd-shaped rocks? No less an expert than Dr. Louis Leakey believed the tools to be authentic, and he supervised the excavation of the site from 1964 until his death in 1972. It's still an active dig, one you can participate in, and it's located about 10 miles east of Ghost Town Road. You can take I-15 to the Minneola Road exit, or remain loyal to the backroads: Turn left out of Calico, follow the road under the interstate, then turn left on the frontage road to Minneola Road. The approach to the Calico Early Man Site is by way of good dirt road.

Stop in first at the visitor center, which is an old miner's shack. The site is open Wednesday through Sunday, with regular guided tours. You can pick up a map for a self-guided tour, but you can't enter the digs without a guide.

Rock or artifact? A guide at Calico Early Man Site points to what might be a stone tool. If so, such finds place man in North America tens of thousands of years before the prevailing opinion of 12,000 years ago.

I recommend the tour. Three master pits have been painstakingly dug out with only awls, dental picks, and fine brushes, then sifted through and cataloged. Master Pit 2 is 26 feet deep. You don a hardhat, then enter the cool depths of the dig. You can see a few rocks sticking out that have sharp edges—nature rounds and abrades rock, but sharp edges indicate the hand of man. Some of the rocks look like they could be scrapers or axes, and a lot look like, well, rocks. Nothing else has been found on the site to indicate human presence.

So who knows? They've found over 12,000 artifacts of significant quality to indicate the presence of *Homo erectus* or *Homo sapiens neanderthalensis* on this site. And you can join in by coming out the first weekend of every month. It doesn't look like as much fun as Indiana Jones always had, but it's for a good cause.

From here, return to I-15. You can go east to Baker and begin Tour 14 of the East Mojave, or west to Barstow and pick up Tour 18, Old Route 66.

Anza-Borrego Desert State Park

150 miles

Anza-Borrego State Park Visitor Center • Borrego Palm Canyon • Borrego Springs • Vallecito Stage Station County Park • Mountain Palm Springs • Ocotillo • Borrego Badlands • Salton City

Anza-Borrego meets every expectation of what a desert should be, yet it's anything but predictable. (I take that back. If you visit in the middle of August, I predict that it will be very hot.) It has all the vastness, loneliness, sere sand, and corrugated badlands that any self-respecting desert should have. But Anza-Borrego also has palm oases that could pass for Bali Hai. It has spring wildflowers in heart-stirring profusion. It has spindly ocotillo cactus—desert comedians that frame vast views of mountains and canyon washes. And it has a human history that brings the present-day traveler to a kinship with those who passed before. Traveling this desert is so obviously difficult—it even challenges an air-conditioned motorist—that the sight of an old stagecoach trail stirs a sympathetic imagination.

This tour takes in most of the principal paved roads of Anza-Borrego, with a couple of dirt-road options that are accessible to two-wheel drive vehicles. With four-wheel-

drive you can range much farther, but it's not at all necessary
to venture off-road to sample the essence of Anza-Borrego.

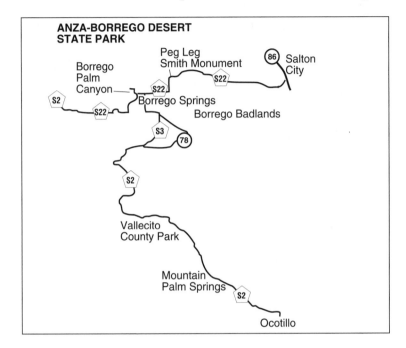

To begin the tour: Take Interstate 10 or State Highway 60
(Pomona Freeway) east from Los Angeles to I-15 south, to
State Highway 79. Follow Highway 79 south to San Diego
County Road S2 (San Felipe Road) to S22 (Montezuma
Valley Road), which leads to park headquarters and the
town of Borrego Springs.

Anza-Borrego State Park is open all year, but winter and
spring are the most popular times to visit when the daytime
highs average in the 70s and 80s. Although the park
receives only about five inches of rain a year, gentle winter
rains fall occasionally between December and March. These
are the all-important "wildflower rains" that ensure the
park's colorful spring pageant. In summer, temperatures
can reach 125 degrees and fierce thunderstorms can fall—

these are the deluges that send flash-floods through the washes. For the most part, weather is delightful from September to June.

In any season, always carry five gallons of water with you in your vehicle, and plenty of water with you on even short hikes. If you're out for a day or more, carry a gallon per person per day. Be sure your car's cooling system is in good order, and be willing to turn off your air conditioner on the longer grades to prevent overheating.

PARK APPROACH

This western approach road to Anza-Borrego is spectacular. Once it begins to drop from a mesa dotted with sage, the road twists down a long, 8-percent grade literally carved out of rock. From a number of viewpoints you get an aerial view of Borrego Springs, looking quite lush amid the arid flatlands, and the vast desert receding eastward toward what

Spindly ocotillo in spring bloom beside Montezuma Valley Road (S-22), the western approach to Anza-Borrego Desert State Park.

looks like a giant, shimmering body of water. This incongruous sight is no mirage, but rather the Salton Sea.

If you make the descent in spring, wildflowers will compete with the vistas for your attention. You know you're in Anza-Borrego when you see the long, looping stalks of green ocotillo arcing 15 or 20 feet and sprouting bright orange-red blossoms. Near Culp Valley, where there's a campground and a vista point, you're likely to see carpets of bright blue lupine, and you'll spot various other showy annuals poking through the rocks. If you surmise that theirs is a hard and tenacious life, you've pretty much summed up the nature of Anza-Borrego.

PARK HEADQUARTERS AND HISTORY

Montezuma Valley Road ultimately deposits you on the floor of Borrego Valley where you should beeline to the state park visitor center. The building is an attraction in itself. Taking a cue from so many animal dwellers of the desert, the visitor center is hewn from the ground, dug right out of a hillside, and given a stone facade. A surrounding cactus garden contains most of the prominent natives you'll be encountering on your Anza-Borrego travels: ocotillo, yucca, agave, brittlebush, smoke trees, elephant trees, and palo verde trees. Docents conduct frequent strolls through the garden to help you match names with faces. Inside are an excellent bookstore, displays on desert plants, wildlife, Indian natives, and western settlers, and an introductory slide show. The visitor center also maintains an up-to-the-minute chart of wildflower blooms and their locations. Wildflower season runs from late February into April. Early March is usually peak time for wildflower viewing. Another chart in the visitor center lists the dirt roads that are currently passable by two-wheel drive.

Anza-Borrego draws its name from a yoking of two symbolic presences in this desert. Juan Bautista de Anza was the

Spanish leader of extraordinary 1774 and 1776 expeditions that passed through this desert on the way from Mexico to Monterey, on the California coast. *Borrego* is the Spanish word for the bighorn sheep, a reticent dweller of the rocky desert canyons and mountains.

Mexican explorers opened up a parallel route to Anza's in 1824, which later brought soldiers, gold-seekers, stage-coach travelers, and even the U.S. Mail across the rugged desert on a course that came to be known as the Southern Emigrant Trail. These white men naturally considered the desert a forbidding place to traverse and exited as quickly as possible. Of course, all the while, tribes of Kumeyaay and Cahuilla Indians lived quite happily in the desert. These seminomadic people placed their temporary villages near water sources, hunted small game, ground flour from mesquite beans and acorns, and utilized desert plants for medicines, clothing, and basketry.

Only recently has modern man begun to understand the desert as a place of beauty and abundance. The Indians' knowledge of the desert and the seeming ease with which they lived in such harsh conditions is depicted in the visitor center. Spending a little time in homage and appreciation of the natives can enhance a visit to Anza-Borrego, the name given their homeland.

At 600,000 acres (approximately 60 miles long and 30 miles wide), Anza-Borrego is among the largest state parks in the country. Created in 1933, it contains most of the west-ern portion of the Colorado Desert.

THE ULTIMATE OASIS

If you have time and energy for only one hike in Anza-Borrego, make it the three-mile round trip to Borrego Palm Canyon. Do it early in the morning, if possible, when you won't have much human company, so you can hear the songs of dozens of bird species and perhaps see some wildlife taking an early morning drink. The trailhead is a mile from park headquarters, in Borrego Palm Canyon Headquarters. As you stairstep up the rocky trail you soon come upon a fresh flowing stream—a mere hint of the lushness that lies ahead. As you approach the head of the canyon, you see a few palms, then a forest of them. You see a few waterfalls, then a 30-foot cascade over smooth granite and green ferns, all shaded by stout fan palms. A songbird soundtrack accompanies the soothing sound of tumbling water, and tiny hummingbirds flit overhead like giant bumblebees. In ambient air that seems to suck moisture from your body (it does, actually), Borrego Palm Canyon is moist and abundant. On the return trip, you can elect to take a longer, higher route back that winds among some huge ocotillo.

The town of Borrego Springs, just east of park headquarters and a private island within the public park, is a mostly unpretentious little burg of about 3,000 residents, perhaps a hint of what Palm Springs might have been like a couple of generations ago. It has several motels, a few restaurants, and a couple of large resorts. Be sure to gas up here—you don't want to venture into the park on a partial tank.

YAQUI PASS AND SCISSORS CROSSING

Our tour leads south out of Borrego Springs on Borrego Springs Road and County Road S3 toward Yaqui Pass. Look closely and you'll see an entire hillside on your left spotted with barrel cactus as you crest, then descend, this rocky divide. At the bottom of the down-grade is Tamarisk Grove Campground, the rare desert camping spot with shade trees and hot showers. Across the road, a short hiking trail called the Cactus Loop leads through a colorful variety of cholla, ocotillo, and barrel cacti.

At Tamarisk Grove, turn right on State Highway 78 toward Julian. You'll soon come to County Road S2, an

So-called "jumping cholla" cactus: Joints easily detach and find their way onto human legs and feet.

intersection known as Scissors Crossing. A historical plaque here marks this as the site of the San Felipe Stage Station, one of the stations that served passengers on the Butterfield Overland Stage route.

SOUTHERN EMIGRANT TRAIL

When you turn left on S2 at Scissors Crossing, you're on the route of Butterfield Overland Stage, known as the Southern Emigrant Trail. Most of the trail is paved over, but a few traces of the original remain. The Butterfield line covered 2,000 miles from Tipton (near St. Louis), Missouri, to San Francisco. The trip took 24 days in the 1850s and 1860s if all went well, and "well" was certainly relative. Stage stations were generally a day's ride apart. Here the driver would exchange horses, and passengers would get a meal and lodging.

"All passengers out!" was a familiar call to hopeful emigrants who paid a good portion of their life savings to make this trip. Whenever the going got too steep, the driver would have to lighten the load. At times the passengers would even have to push the coach. One such obligatory debarking was at Foot and Walker Pass, and you can easily

The trail to the left of this historical monument (near S2 in Blair Valley) led through Foot and Walker Pass, one of the most difficult passages of the Butterfield Overland stage route. Passengers had to debark and help push their coach here.

see the spot. After mile marker 22, turn left into Blair Valley and follow the good dirt road about a half-mile. Turn left again at a yellow marker for the California Riding and Hiking Trail, and park. You'll see a short, steep, rocky path—it's unimaginable that even unloaded stagecoaches could ascend it. Walk 150 feet up the pass and you'll find a historical monument near the top.

Blair Valley has other historical sites if you're up for some dirt-road adventuring. Beyond the Butterfield site, it's one of those roads you should check on at the visitor center, but it's generally passable by two-wheel drive. Along the way are: Ghost Mountain, where Marshal South built an adobe home and raised a family in the 1930s (it's a steep, one-mile hike to the home site); the Morteros, holes in granite boulders used by native women to grind seeds and pods; and the Pictograph Trail (the road gets pretty rutted this last mile and a half), where another one-mile hiking trail leads to some fine examples of Indian rock art.

Another moving site that depicts the difficulties of the early travelers is Box Canyon, beyond mile marker 25, where there's a signed overlook. It's easy to see the dead-end the first wagons here encountered and the trail they built to get around it. Soldiers of the Mormon Battalion carved the alternate route out of solid rock with only axes and a pry bar.

As you continue south on S2, you drop into a succession of lower valleys. As you descend the Campbell Grade, you can clearly see a trail of wagon ruts across the desert floor. This valley contains a virtual forest of ocotillo interspersed with tall agave stalks. Agave, or century plants, were a mainstay in Indian life. The Indians roasted the white base of the plant, fermented the sap, made rope and sandals from the fibers, and used the long stalks to construct roofs.

Next stop down the trail is the Vallecito Stage Station, a San Diego County park. The station was built in 1852 and restored in 1934. It's not technically adobe, but rather made of bricks cut from a nearby saltgrass marsh. The bricks contained mud and roots. Builders would water down the bricks as they built so the roots would continue growing and bind the bricks together into a very solid construction. It's cool inside the thick walls—what a welcome rest stop this must have been for stage passengers. It's also surprisingly clean, considering the mud walls and dirt floor. The floor is so hard that it can be swept, even mopped. A guide told me that adding cow urine to the floor helped solidify it. Surrounding the restored station are mesquite trees, indicating the presence of permanent water. A picnic area and campground are adjacent to the station.

Below Vallecito, the paved road and the stage route diverge. The stage line made a difficult course across the Carrizo Badlands, which you can see from the Carrizo Corridor Overlook at mile marker 43. A better viewpoint is another eight miles down the road.

As an oasis, Mountain Palm Springs, just past mile marker 47, is not as teeming with life as Borrego Palm Canyon; but in any of its seven palm groves, it's easy to find isolation and serenity—just you and the birds. The nearest is a half-mile from the parking area.

Two of seven distinct palm groves are a short walk from the campground/parking area in Mountain Palm Springs. Palms signify the presence of water and draw abundant bird and animal life.

Below Mountain Palm Springs, the road makes a zigzag climb out of the valley and up Sweeney Pass to the Carrizo Badlands Overlook, a half-mile south of mile marker 51. Badlands are what gives the desert an ominous reputation. For miles, the desert floor is a maze of twisted, gnarled, wind-eroded sedimentary layers. Just below the overlook, a four-wheel drive road leads into the badlands via Canyon Sin Nombre (Canyon Without a Name). It's easy enough to walk three-fourths of a mile into this canyon, which imparts a powerful sense of isolation amid a dramatically exposed palimpsest of geology.

Split rocks are a common geological phenomenon in Anza-Borrego, this one in Canyon Sin Nombre.

From here, it's 4.5 miles to the state park's southern border, then another eight miles to the small town of Ocotillo and Interstate 8. Because there's no way to fashion a loop in Anza-Borrego, you'll need to retrace your way 56 miles to Borrego Springs to continue the tour of the park. You'll be surprised how different the scenery looks in the reverse direction.

If it's late in the day and you're not camping, I suggest you drive west on I-8 about 15 miles to the Jacumba exit, then proceed on Old Highway 80 to the tiny town of Jacumba. Jacumba was literally left in the dust by I-8 and the closing of the railroad, but it's a tenacious little place with a couple of stores and the charming Jacumba Hot Springs Spa/Motel/Restaurant. Here you can bathe or swim in natural mineral waters and enjoy a good meal. To show you how informal things are in Jacumba, the Mexican border just south of town is a wire gate. Residents of the village of Jacame, Mexico, simply open the gate and stroll up a dirt road to shop in Jacumba. They're seven miles from the nearest paved road in Mexico, so it's easier this way and no one seems to mind.

THE BORREGO-SALTON SEAWAY

Once you've retraced the 56 miles back to Borrego Springs, turn right (east) on S22. This is a good road that crosses the Borrego Badlands, built in 1968 to replace a hand-hewn track called the Truckhaven Trail. The new road reduced travel time between Borrego Springs and Salton City from four hours to a half-hour. But don't try to make it in a half-hour, because you'll want to make a few stops along the way.

Pause first at the Peg Leg Monument, where the road makes a 90-degree bend and the Borrego-Salton Seaway begins. The monument memorializes Peg Leg Smith, a wanderer who showed up circa 1829, picked up some rocks in this vicinity, and carried them with him to Los Angeles where he was told they were pure gold. For some reason, Peg Leg didn't beeline back to Borrego Valley until 1850. By then, his memory had faded a bit, or maybe he was just unlucky. Despite repeated attempts to find his lost mine, Peg Leg came up empty. But he was always a good yarn-spinner, so Smith managed to make a living talking about gold rather than mining it. He helped to create his own folk legend, which lives on today. In fact, an annual gathering called the Peg Leg Liar's Contest takes place at this site on the first Saturday in April—exaltation of the art of the tall story.

A huge rock pile has formed at the site of the monument because a sign proclaims, "Let him who seeks Peg Leg Smith's gold add 10 rocks to the monument." A register inside a rural mailbox beside the rock pile makes good reading. Most entries are a variation on how the visitor found Peg Leg's gold but decided to leave it. The mailbox is also a repository for the recirculating of magazines and paperbacks among desert rats.

As you proceed east, you face the Santa Rosa Mountains. Pull over at the Santa Rosa Overlook for a good look. This sudden upthrust of a mountain range represents the most active earthquake fault in California, a branch of the San Andreas Fault. The mountains rise over 8,000 feet from the floor of Clark Valley and Clark Dry Lake, which you can see clearly several miles ahead. Every once in awhile, when flood waters seep into this ancient lakebed, tiny shrimp hatch from drought-resistant eggs as if touched into brief life by a fairy's wand. The shrimp grow quickly to their full, one-inch size, lay eggs, and die. The cycle can take years to repeat.

The best badlands view in the park is at Font's Point. The turnoff is just past mile marker 29 for this four-mile dirt road, but it may not be passable for two-wheel-drive vehicles. The condition of the road is posted in the park visitor center. But don't worry; you can stay on the paved road and still see the badlands very well. At mile marker 34, the road begins a remarkable crossing of the Borrego Badlands. A paved turnout yields a fine view and makes one marvel at the task of building this road across these eerily eroded, dry-mud hills. This was once a huge lakebed, then a steamy savannah, and its mud and clay deposits have been uplifted by faulting and eroded by wind to create the present badlands. These canyons and washes roar with torrential flash floodwaters during violent summer storms.

The park brochure states something that becomes obvious when you visit Anza-Borrego State Park—that despite recent discoveries of fossil mammals, early man sites, and new species, "all that is known about Anza-Borrego is barely a scratch on the surface of the information that still lies hidden in the canyons, on the high ridges, and beneath the ancient sediments of this wilderness park." This tour has barely scratched the scratches on the surface. Visiting at a different time of year can be an entirely different experience of the same itinerary. Or taking new trails, or more time to explore familiar ones, can reveal hidden dimensions of a place that cannot be fully explored, even in a lifetime.

You'll continue crossing badlands after you exit the park, and soon after crossing Imperial County Line you'll get a good view of the Salton Sea. Then the road dips down below sea level and ends at State Highway 86 in Salton City. From here you can pick up Tour 17 for a loop around the Salton Sea or follow Highway 86 north to Interstate 10.

A Salton Sea Loop

150 miles
*North Shore • Salton Sea State Recreation Area • Niland
• Slab City • Brawley • Salton City • Coachella • Indio*

Don't come to the Salton Sea expecting anything conventionally "beautiful." You might find some glimmers of beauty, or you might be overwhelmed by the utter bleakness of the place. So to enjoy this loop drive around the Salton Sea, it helps to cultivate a fascination for the area's strange history and quirky geography. Much of the desert that surrounds it is of the sparse type that gives deserts a bad name, and few tourists would forsake Palm Springs anytime soon for Salton Sea communities. Even at the shoreline, where lakes normally engender a degree of riparian verdancy, the Salton Sea seems scruffy at best, lifeless at worst.

But to leathery old salts who live or fish here and to snowbirds who come in their recreational vehicles to escape the bone-chilling cold of northern latitudes, it's probably paradise personified. And I do think there's a certain aesthetic appeal to the area if you're there at the right time and squint your eyes just a bit to soften some rough edges. But the real reason I like the Salton Sea is because it's so darn *odd*. It's like a sympathetic science-fiction monster: It was created by accident, is more mineral-laden than the

Pacific Ocean, lies out there simmering in the sun in a below-sea-level sink that gets 2.4 inches of rain a year, and yet the thing is getting bigger all the time. And despite a very bare midriff, all sorts of things are growing near its north and south shores. What's going on here?

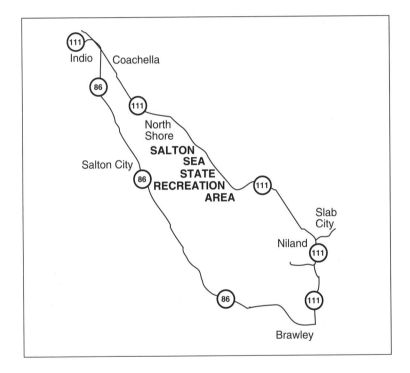

To begin the tour: Take Interstate 10 east from Los Angeles to State Highway 86/111 south in Indio. Continue south on Highway 111 through Coachella and Mecca toward the town of North Shore.

As you approach the Salton Sea, you'll notice a great variety of agriculture—the miracles of modern irrigation — along its northern environs. You'll see groves of date palms and citrus, farm workers' shacks, fish farms, and a lot of flat, open space. Maybe it's just power of suggestion, knowing that you're below sea level, but the air feels rich, dense, and heavy.

NORTH SHORE

North Shore isn't much of a town, nor are any of the "seaside" settlements here. Ruins of marinas, motels, restaurants, and apartment buildings testify to faded dreams and speculative schemes that went nowhere. Mobile home courts and RV parks seem to be the only developments that could take root around this briny shore. Just south of what town there is are the headquarters, marina, and main campground for the Salton Sea State Recreation Area and one of the few places where there's much human action near the shore. Ski boats and fishermen launch from the marina, and shaded picnic tables provide an opportunity to watch the "action."

In the fading light of dusk, the north shore of the Salton Sea can take on the guise of paradise, although the scene belies the barrenness of most of the shoreline.

THE ACCIDENTAL SEA

A hundred years ago, the large depression filled by the Salton Sea was bone dry. So was the Imperial Valley below it, which was a situation some speculators of the 1890s wanted to correct. They theorized that the soil of the area, composed of ancient silt from the Colorado River, would be fertile for agriculture—if only they could water it. A promoter and engineer named Charles Rockwood spearheaded a system of canals that tapped Colorado River water for the valley. By 1904, 700 miles of canals irrigated 77,000 acres of cultivated land.

But all this playing God with the river backfired. First, Colorado River silt (it carried 10 tons of silt for every acre-foot of water) blocked the main canal, and the Imperial Valley's pipes went dry. A bypass canal was cut, which promptly silted up, then another—same story. Then the developers made a temporary cut across the border in Mexico, where water would flow while they dredged the main canal. They didn't foresee an early spring that year, but snow in the Rockies melted early, and the Colorado's flood stage was higher than normal. The river went on a rampage, made quick work of the temporary channel, and happily made for the Salton Sink. Imperial Valley settlers could do nothing but nervously watch the river flood the low-lying basin. A lake was born. (Not unprecedented—an ancient, much larger lake once filled the sink. You can plainly see traces of its shoreline if you look to the hills beyond the perimeter of the present-day sea.) No one objected to the lake's being there, but how soon would it take over their fertile farmland? A succession of heroic efforts failed to stop the flow.

Finally, in early 1908, Southern Pacific Railroad (sensing that its lucrative business in the Imperial Valley could be wiped out) succeeded in building a trestle and proceeded to dump thousands of boxcars of rock into the river. It was a race—would the river make matchsticks of the trestle before enough rock could be dumped in front of it to return the river to its course? Finally, a lull in the flow and a mad-paced effort succeeded. The Colorado was tamed, and skulked off to the Gulf of California, leaving behind the Salton Sea as a giant souvenir of its rebellious period.

STATE PARK SHORELINE

Although created by fresh water, the Salton Sea is 10 percent "saltier" than the Pacific Ocean. Its mineral composition, however, is actually different. Four types of fish manage to live in the heavily mineralized Salton Sea water: corvina, croaker, sargo, and talapia. The toothy corvina is the sportiest of the lot and ranges from three to 30 pounds. Many other species have been introduced over the years, but it takes a hardy fish to survive here—the sea is becoming progressively more mineralized as agricultural runoffs pour into it. Evaporation continually increases the concentration of the minerals. It takes a hardy breed of sportfishers, too. It seems that fishing gets better from spring right into summer when the water heats up to 90 degrees and the daytime high might be 115 to 120. (But, as they say, it's "dry" heat.)

The next 14 miles of shoreline are state park, with several campgrounds along the way. The immediate surroundings aren't what you'd call lush—just a few scattered creosote bushes—but the rugged Chocolate Mountains add texture to your view to the east and south, and you can see the Santa Rosas rising through the haze across the sea. Bombay Beach does nothing to enhance the setting; it's a curious jumble of decaying mobile homes, cars, and boats in various states of disrepair and a few landscaped homes.

Finally, as you approach Niland, a few irrigated farms appear to the east and some curious puffs of smoke to the south. More about those later.

SLAB CITY

Niland is a real town with a couple of stores, cafes, and gas stations and an annual Tomato Festival, but its most noteworthy institution is a sociological phenomenon known as Slab City. It's been likened to a hippie commune for seniors, this abandoned Marine Corps installation just east of Niland, where thousands of RVers come every winter to park their motorhomes and trailers for free, to soak weary bones in sunshine, and to enjoy the informal camaraderie of the place. Slab City has no facilities at all, but a government of sorts has developed among the snowbirds. They handle such matters as waste disposal and water dispersement themselves.

The first left in Niland, Beal Road, leads out to Slab City. As you approach, you can see that the snowbirds' spiritual needs are also taken care of. Salvation Mountain is a big dirt pile at the entrance to the Slabs that has been concreted, painted brightly, and inscribed with religious slogans. "God is Love" stands out in 10-foot letters. Among the con-

Salvation Mountain, a concreted dike at the entrance to The Slabs, is a makeshift religious shrine to welcome RV snowbirds to their makeshift winter home.

crete slabs left behind by the Marines, folks walk little dogs, huddle under shade awnings, or hawk second-hand goods. Imperial County is always making noises about cracking down on Slab City, but the seniors have managed to fend off the bureaucrats for many years.

REAL SNOWBIRDS

The snowbirds of Slab City have counterparts just a few miles away. Real snowbirds migrate to certain sections of the Salton Sea shore in huge numbers. In winter, as many as 20,000 Canada geese and snow geese may congregate in a single pond, marsh, or field in the Salton Sea National Wildlife Refuge just south of Niland. (Turn west on Sinclair Road from Highway 111.) Refuge headquarters is located here, where you can pick up a bird list (380 species have been sighted in the refuge) and see some waterfowl exhibits. Even if it's not prime time for migratory birds, a walk out on Rock Hill Trail will stir up a few snipes, plovers, red-winged blackbirds, orioles, and maybe some herons and egrets. The sound you hear akin to a tuba

A great blue heron skims across the placid sea. In winter, the Salton Sea National Wildlife Refuge draws tens of thousands of migratory birds.

rehearsal is the call of numerous bullfrogs. The trail culminates in a rise overlooking the sea and the fields around the refuge that are cultivated strictly for the birds (keeps them from invading nearby farms). In winter, the phenomenon of thousands of snow geese simultaneously flapping their black-tipped wings literally stirs the air as they rise slowly off the water, in outline against the snow-capped Santa Rosas. It's enough to give you goosebumps.

Also from the refuge you'll get a close look at the rising puffs of smoke you saw earlier. These are geothermal power plants that generate electricity (and a lot of noise) from the heat of relatively shallow, underground magma in this area, which also heats some mud pots (around the Wister Waterfowl Management Area north of Niland) and mineral baths (spas near Bombay Beach).

BRAWLEY TO SALTON CITY

As you continue south toward Brawley from the refuge, it's a startling contrast to the barren desert just a few miles north. Here are vast fields of carrots, lettuce, cantaloupe, and huge feed lots for cattle. Brawley, for all its agriculture, is really a cow town and celebrates an annual Cattle Call and Rodeo in November. It has an old-fashioned downtown dominated by the huge old Planters Hotel, which seems to be nothing but a cocktail lounge now. In downtown Brawley you'll turn right on State Highway 78/86 (Main Street) to begin the swing north around the west side of the Salton Sea.

West of the small town of Westmoreland you can turn on Vendel Road and follow it nine miles to another unit of the Salton Sea National Wildlife Refuge. Otherwise, continue on Highway 78/86, leaving agriculture behind and returning to barren desert and, on the west, the badlands that extend from Anza-Borrego Desert State Park. Highway 78 diverges west into the park. Stay on Highway 86 and continue to Salton City.

Salton City is a strange blend of resort and ghost town. Again, it's the mobile home and RV developments that seem to succeed. Big motels and restaurants stand empty, parched, and fading. On your left, a few miles north, is another indicator of past life—Travertine Rock. This large rock beside the highway was once an island in the lake that was the forerunner of the Salton Sea. You can see travertine, or tufa, deposits (calcium carbonate) laced with tiny snail and mussel shells on the portion of the rock that was below water, and higher up you'll see where wave action scrubbed off the rock's desert varnish.

DATE CAPITAL

You may or may not have noticed that the climate of the Salton trough closely resembles that of southern Algeria. Thanks to this fortuitous fact, the Coachella Valley is the date capital of the New World. The vast shady groves of date palms rustling in the breeze beneath the Santa Rosa Mountains are another product of vision and ingenuity. Officials of our own Department of Agriculture were responsible for the experiments early in the century that proved the viability of date cultivation in the Coachella Valley. Then early settlers in the harsh, hot valley banded together in a cooperative to purchase the Deglet Noor offshoots from Algeria that still account for the vast majority of Coachella Valley dates.

Each acre of 48 date palms has one male to preside over a harem of females, which produce the fruit. Growers have to hand-cultivate each female tree every year, and later cover each bunch of dates with a paper "umbrella" to protect them from dust, rain, birds, and insects until they are picked in the fall.

Early in the century, agricultural experts realized that the Salton Sea/Coachella Valley climate resembled that of southern Algeria. They theorized that date palms could flourish, and they were right.

As you drive north on Highway 86 into Coachella and Indio, you'll pass through huge date gardens and a number of streetside date stands. The valley is renowned for grapefruit as well, and in some groves you see grapefruit trees interspersed with tall date palms as if being protected by big brothers. One of the oldest date centers in the valley is the Covaldo Date Company, still housed in its whitewashed building beside Highway 86 in Coachella. It's kind of a date-themed cultural center as well as produce market and date-packing plant. Here you can sample the plump Deglet Nools and some exotic varieties of dates, buy gift boxes for shipping, see displays about date cultivation and harvesting, and, if the plant's in operation, watch dates being packed for shipment. I must admit I'm not much for dates, but the soft, moist, fresh ones plucked right from an Indio date garden are a far cry from the desiccated junk we get in supermarkets. I also enjoy Covaldo's selection of out-of-print postcards—old cards, once intended to entice, that make the Salton Sea look considerably more forlorn than it is.

Numerous roadside stands sell dates and date products. Covalda Date Co. in Coachella is more than a stand; it's also a packing house and virtually a shrine to Coachella Valley dates.

At the junction of Highways 86 and 111, turn left on Highway 111 into Indio. On your left you'll see an exotic-looking complex called the Desert Expo Centre. This is the site of the National Date Festival/Riverside County Fair every February. With an Arabian Nights sub-theme and events like ostrich and camel races, this is unlike any other county fair. Beyond the Expo Centre you'll find more big date shops. Jensen's has a showcase garden, and Shield's presents a slide show on the history of dates.

By now you're in the heart of civilization once again, such as it is. At times, as you pass through the golf-course and fast-food wonderland, you might find yourself missing the undeveloped authenticity, the quirkiness, and the just plain oddness of the Salton Sea.

Highway 111 leads through the resort towns of the Coachella Valley and into Palm Springs. You can follow it this way to State Highway 74 and pick up Tour 8 and the Palms-to-Pines Highway in reverse, or follow it all the way to Interstate 10. You can also turn north up a number of streets that lead more directly to Interstate 10 for the return to Los Angeles.

TOUR 18

Route 66

270 miles
*Goffs • Amboy • Newberry Springs • Barstow •
Victorville • San Bernardino • Pasadena • Santa Monica*

Route 66 is both a backroad and a ghost road, a nostalgic reprise of an era when automobile journeys were fueled by dreams. U.S. Highway 66, once dubbed "America's Main Street," cut an arcing slice through the heartland of America, stretching 2,448 miles from Chicago to the beach in Santa Monica. It was the pride of the national highway system, even though it was little more than a signed series of pathways and rutted farm roads when christened in 1926, and wasn't fully paved until 1938.

The development of Route 66 paralleled, probably spurred, the growth of pleasure driving in America. The California dream drew travelers westward (Los Angeles doubled in population between 1920 and 1930), and they needed services along the way. What ensued was quintessentially American: Motels lured travelers with art-deco neon. So did coffee shops and roadside restaurants. Curio shops and trading posts extracted tourist dollars. Billboards and barn-sides touted coming attractions. Gas stations were needed, and they sprang up everywhere. So did tire shops, and wreckers did bonanza business. One watering-hole town in the middle of the Mojave Desert supported no fewer than seven wreckers.

During the dust-bowl '30s, thousands of Joad-type families arrived in California via Route 66, living out *Grapes of Wrath* lives. Novelist John Steinbeck called it "the mother road." In the wartime '40s, military traffic dominated. After the war, songwriter Bobby Troup decided to have a go at Hollywood, and on his way west wrote a song called "Get Your Kicks on Route 66." Nat King Cole recorded it, and the mythical stature of the highway grew along with the notion that the journey was as meaningful as the destination and that a two-lane ribbon of tarmac and concrete could have personality, even life.

Even as roadside business boomed in the 1950s, the death knell for Route 66 was sounding. In 1956, Congress passed the Interstate Highway Act. In the early '60s, the *Route 66* television series kept the mystique alive. But a growing country demanded the speed and efficiency that limited-access highways could provide. It took nearly 30 years, but eventually, Route 66 was replaced by not one, but five interstates: 55, 44, 40, 15, and 10. In 1985, the year when the last form of concrete was poured on Interstate 40 near Williams, Arizona, the last of the official shield-shaped "U.S. 66" signs were taken down.

But matters dear to the American heart have a way of enduring. Local and national Route 66 associations keep the course and, to an extent, the spirit of Route 66 alive. Some segments of the original road remain, forlorn, dusty, bypassed by parallel megahighways. Other sections are main streets through suburban communities. Others, of course, rest in peace beneath multiple lanes of modern-day freeways. No one accords an interstate highway much in the way of personality. To find that, to find what's left of the substance and spirit of Route 66, you have to exit, drive a little slower, and keep your eyes and imagination open.

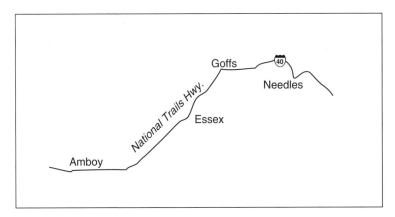

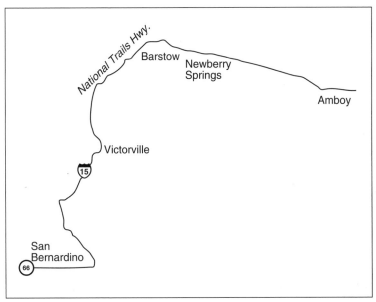

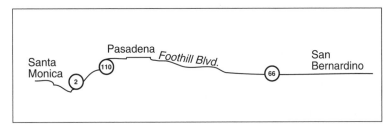

Which, of course, is the spirit of this book. So even though much of modern-day Route 66 is anything but backroad, other stretches are as fun to drive as grandma's attic is fun to explore. Many facsimile signs, some just painted on plywood, help you follow the route through the Mojave, through the foothill suburbs, through Los Angeles to the Pacific.

It only seems fitting to trace the California remnants of Route 66 from east to west, the same direction in which American dreams have so long flowed, the way most Route 66 immigrants arrived. So this tour works perfectly as a return route from a tour of the East Mojave (see Tour 14).

To begin the tour: Exit Interstate 40 at U.S. Highway 95 ten miles west of Needles and turn left, west, on Old Route 66, which parallels the railroad tracks. Or, if you've been traveling the East Mojave, join Old Route 66 in Goffs or Essex.

GOFFS TO NEWBERRY SPRINGS

The long, lonely Mojave section of Old Route 66 is a classic country drive that vividly conjures the Old 66 experience. As it follows telephone lines and railroad tracks in long straight stretches, it's patched with bumpy mosaics of tar and runs by ghostly ruins of old cafes and gas stations—and, happily, a few stubborn survivors that eke out a living catering to nostalgia buffs and lost travelers.

Until recently, the cafe/gas station/store at Goffs was one of those survivors. It was closed and boarded up at press time, looking for a buyer. For now, it's a pay phone, a public thermometer, and an empty ice machine.

Continue toward Fenner and Essex, cross under I-40, and join the National Old Trails Highway, a pre-66 designation. The presence of a tree or two usually heralds the presence of a lonely house, and the presence of a house usually means a

A few original road signs remain along remote stretches of Route 66, here between Goffs and Fenner.

few dozen hulls of old cars and piles of tires. Car corpses and tractor tires are a prevailing theme along the old road.

In the "town" of Essex, a tree partially obscures a sign, so the cafe seems to be marked "Sex Cafe." Essex also has an old stone post office, still in use, and a gas station, which isn't. And there's no shortage of car carcasses. On the edge of town, the Smith family advertises Route 66 souvenirs for sale—mostly road signs, license plates, and, you guessed it, old wrecked cars.

From Essex to Cadiz Summit, if you like to count telephone poles or creosote bushes, you're in luck. There's a steady supply of both. This is the kind of road where a car with a good wheel alignment can drive itself. At the summit, a rocky rise in the road, are the ruins of what seem to be an old viewing tower and maybe a cafe.

An occasional palo verde tree is all that catches the eye until Chambless, where an empty restaurant/market/gas station is of more recent vintage than some other Route 66 ruins, but just as abandoned. Across the street is a plaque honoring Route 66.

At last, in Amboy, you come to a living entity: Roy's Motel and Cafe, serving highway travelers since 1945. Traffic on Route 66 once supported seven wreckers working out of Amboy. Today, the occasional straggler wanders in for a cold drink, a soft bed, or a souvenir t-shirt.

Just outside of Amboy, on the south side of the road, is Amboy Crater, a volcanic cinder cone that spewed the dark lava that surrounds it. A very bumpy dirt road leads to a footpath that ascends the cinder cone.

If you blink you'll miss the ruins of the town of Bagdad, the place that inspired the wonderfully quirky movie *Bagdad Cafe*. Don't despair—the actual cafe used in the movie is down the road in Newberry Springs.

In Ludlow are an abandoned cafe and numerous abandoned shacks, but two (count 'em) working gas stations. The metropolitan trappings are due to the presence of I-40. Old 66 crosses under the interstate here and follows the north side for awhile before it ducks under again at Pisgah, site of another volcanic cinder cone. A mine of sorts on the

Ghostly hulls of old cars are common souvenirs along Route 66.

west side of the crater extracts the kind of crushed cinder you may use in your garden.

BAGDAD CAFE

In Newberry Springs, the Sidewinder Cafe is humble, unpretentious, and serves up good food, like real milk-shakes, burgers, and liver-and-onions. It starred in the 1987 movie *Bagdad Cafe* (with Jack Palance and Marianne Sagebrecht) as a friendly place in the middle of nowhere, which it pretty much is. It didn't even occur to the owners to change the name to draw in movie buffs, although it does anyway—the cafe is a sleepy mecca of sorts for fans from around the world who have seen the movie. On one wall inside is a framed montage of snapshots from the Sidewinder's day in the sun, but the cafe deserves a stop for its own merits.

All along Route 66 you've been playing tag with the Santa Fe Railroad. It seems like Newberry Springs is the place where boxcars and cabooses go when they die—from here to Daggett you'll see a number of them that have been converted into residences.

Daggett was once a bustling railroad town and shipping center for the borax trade. Today its claim to fame is a Marine Corps depot, which forces travelers off the old road and onto I-40 as far as Barstow.

BARSTOW TO VICTORVILLE

Old Route 66 seems positively metropolitan through Barstow, once the site of the busiest gas station in the country, thanks to Route 66 travelers. Take the first exit off I-40 and proceed west through town on Main Street, well marked as Historic Route 66. A few vestiges of the old way remain here, such as $16-a-night motel rooms. Well outside of town, the road continues to be called Main Street, so the signs bring a chuckle—Main Street in the middle of nowhere.

The route swings south now, paralleling Interstate 15, and passes through Lenwood, where a ghostly old drive-in movie screen stands, and Helendale, where the Mojave River irrigates fields of alfalfa and Mount Baldy comes into view. Oro Grande seems to be nothing but a string of abandoned storefronts until you come to Stubbs Auction, a wonderful jumble sale of antique road signs, junk, and treasures.

On the outskirts of Victorville, the road crosses an old steel-lattice bridge, under which the Mojave River makes a rare, above-ground appearance.

VICTORVILLE TO SAN BERNARDINO

In Victorville, Route 66 crosses under I-15 and follows D Street and the railroad tracks into the old part of town, then swings right on 7th Street. The old-fashioned downtown quickly gives way to the world of modern-day franchises, and you realize you've suddenly left the past, and most traces of its old routes and ways, behind. You can continue along all the fast-food joints and shopping centers and join I-15 at Bear Valley Road. Or, better, turn right on LaPaz, hit the freeway, and stop in at the Roy Rogers and Dale Evans Museum. You can't miss it: It's the only building around with a huge statue out front of Trigger reared back on his hind feet.

The museum is like a giant family photo album and the Roy Rogers attic put on display. It's a shame there's no video screen to show some of the old shows or movies, but there's still plenty here to stir memories—best of all, Trigger and Buttermilk themselves, Roy and Dale's beloved horses, stuffed and displayed for eternity.

Most of Route 66 from Victorville to San Bernardino is covered by I-15, but one section of the old road remains through the Cajon Pass. The exit (Cleghorn Road) is well

Whatever this sign referred to was long ago abandoned and overgrown in a lonely and forgotten stretch of Route 66 in Cajon Pass.

marked as Historic Route 66. It's a nifty little remnant route that leaves the din and pace of the interstate quickly behind. Those rocks off to the right are called the Mormon Rocks, big megaliths displaced by the San Andreas Fault which runs right through this pass.

SAN BERNARDINO TO SANTA MONICA

You'll soon be forced back on to the interstate. To stay with the old road, take the Devore exit and follow Cajon Boulevard south, which becomes Mount Vernon Avenue. A few motel ruins and a few old motels still in business—places with names like Capri and Oasis—are about the only reminders of the old route along these bleak San Bernardino city streets.

Route 66 now turns west on 5th Street, which becomes Foothill Boulevard. The Wigwam Motel in Rialto looks like a strange archeological site—some 18 huge stucco tepees

Wigwam Motel in Rialto recalls busier days along Route 66, when it helped to have a gimmick to lure overnight travelers.

that must have lured in a lot of highway travelers in the old days. The motel is pretty worn around the edges, but still in business.

The Wigwam is a fun sight, but once you hit San Bernardino, Route 66 ceases to be anything like a backroad. For the most part, it traces Foothill Boulevard through the Pomona Valley and San Gabriel Mountains foothill communities and involves a lot of stop-and-go driving. You might want to simply jump on I-10 to its terminus at the Pacific Ocean. But determined Route 66 buffs will find signs that point the way through and a few pockets of nostalgia here and there—the 1848 Sycamore Inn in Rancho Cucamonga, the 1926 Aztec Hotel in Monrovia, and the graceful business district of Pasadena.

From Pasadena, take the Arroyo Seco Parkway (State Highway 110) to the Pasadena Freeway, to the westbound Hollywood Freeway (101), to the Santa Monica Boulevard exit. Follow Santa Monica Boulevard west all the way

The Aztec Hotel in Monrovia, built in 1926, is a classic example of architecture clamoring for attention along old Route 66.

through Hollywood, West Hollywood, Beverly Hills, Century City, and West Los Angeles, to Santa Monica.

Road's end is Ocean Boulevard in Santa Monica. A bluffside park overlooks the ocean, and the nearby pier is alluringly tawdry. Panhandlers and homeless people will jar you into the present. But it's also easy to squint a bit, look at the eternal Pacific, and vicariously feel what so many used to feel at the end of Route 66: that you've arrived at the end of the rainbow. What now?

Index

Bold type indicates photograph

214